Books by George A. Sheehan, M.D.

ENCYCLOPEDIA OF ATHLETIC MEDICINE (1972)

DR. SHEEHAN ON RUNNING (1975)

RUNNING AND BEING (1978)

MEDICAL ADVICE FOR RUNNERS (1978)

THIS RUNNING LIFE (1980)

This Running Life

George A. Sheehan, M.D.

SIMON AND SCHUSTER
NEW YORK

Designed by Eve Kirch
Manufactured in the United States of America

1   2   3   4   5   6   7   8   9   10

Library of Congress Cataloging in Publication Data

Sheehan, George.
    This running life.
    1. Running—Psychological aspects.   I. Title.
GV1061.S53   796.4'26   80-15804

ISBN 0-671-25608-4

To my readers who have thought what I have thought, felt what I have felt, and already know what I attempt here to put into words

Contents

Part One

The Body

In the olden days of radio a famous show called "Duffy's Tavern" featured a bartender-philosopher named Archie. One of Archie's patrons was Finnegan, an amiable, simple-minded character, who would greet Archie with the question: "How are things in the world, Arch?" The reply, from a man who knew men and had seen all kinds, was "Your world or ours, Finnegan?"

In a sense, each of us is Finnegan. We each occupy a different world, a world that is separate and distinct from any other. "No two men," writes philospher Maurice Friedman, "are ever in the same situation." Each brings a unique body-mind-spirit totality to his decisions about life's values and his own various options.

Three decades ago, psychologist William Sheldon developed a system for classifying human differences. According to Sheldon, each person could be pinpointed on a chart in relation to three physical and three closely related psychological components. Sheldon gave the physical components the names of *endomorphy* (predominantly soft and rounded), *mesomorphy* (hard, big-boned and strong-muscled) and *ectomorphy* (slender and small-boned with stringy, weak muscles).

The endomorph leans psychologically toward

viscerotonia: love of food, ceremoniousness, childhood and family, sociability and people. The mesomorph's temperament is *somatotonic*. He loves muscular activity, is aggressive, indifferent to pain, courageous, competitive and needs action when in trouble. The ectomorph is *cerebrotonic*. His world is mental. He wants to live and let live. He is nervous, shy, moody, inhibited. He hates loud noises and the bellowing of the mesomorph, and has no patience with the endomorph's love of luxury and ceremony.

Yet daily we endomorphs, mesomorphs and ectomorphs ignore these differences, and insist on asking other people how things are in our own private, personal, never-to-be-duplicated worlds. We are told the absolute, immutable truth in sports, politics, religion and art by people who never warn us: "Your world or ours, Finnegan?"

These same people guide us into mess after mess. We find ourselves at a play we dislike, a movie we can't stand, reading a book that puts us to sleep or secretely enjoying a game that others consider a waste of time. Even with recognized masterpieces, the range of public reaction may extend from one pole to the other, from adoration to repulson. Yet, oddly enough, the people with similar body builds have similar reactions.

Of course we need experts. There is too much to see and know without the help of experienced observers. But we must choose them well. There are times when I'm convinced that if you don't pick a rabbi, priest or minister with your own body statistics, you may end up wishing you were an

Basic Temperamental Traits

Viscerotonia- endomorphy (Circular type)	Somatotonia- mesomorphy (Triangular type)	Cerebrotonia- ectomorphy (Linear type)
Dependent	Dominant	Detached
Relaxed	Assertive	Tense
Calm	Confident	Anxious
Kind	Aggressive	Considerate
Love of comfort	Love of risk	Love of privacy
Extrovert of affect	Extrovert of action	Introvert
Extensive rapport	Enduring rapport	Intensive rapport
Cheerful-depressed	Even-explosive	Hypersensitive-apathetic
Self-satisfied	Self-assured	Self-centered
Soft-tempered	Quick-tempered	Gentle-tempered
Complacent	Irascible	Reflective
Amiable	Talkative	Reserved
Warm	Active	Cool
Affected	Reckless	Suspicious
Tolerant	Energetic	Inhibited
Generous	Enterprising	Restrained
Forgiving	Outgoing	Precise
Needs people when disturbed	Needs action when disturbed	Needs solitude when disturbed
Stress on being	Stress on doing	Stress on perceiving
Lets things happen	Makes things happen	Watches things happen

atheist. That if you don't choose a movie critic with your own bone structure you'll miss the two pictures a year worth seeing.

"Life," wrote Ortega, "is a desperate struggle to succeed in being in fact what we are in design." Design is the word. What we are in design—bone, muscle and gut—determines our temperament and even our values.

In *Varieties of Human Values*, William Morris reports on a study in which different life styles were offered to students of all races and cultures. Surprisingly, he found that those people sharing the same body builds—whether Japanese, Danish, Indian, American or Canadian—opted for the same values. This suggests that the ectomorphic American distance runner relates much better to his foreign counterparts than to his nextdoor neighbors.

Me? I'm five feet, ten inches, weigh 135 pounds and have the bones of a chicken. That's the world you'll read about in this book.

1

The Design

I was born a coward and by any normal standards still am one.

Function follows structure, says the rule of biology, and I don't have the structure to fulfill the function of the red-blooded American male. We all know what that function is: to face up to bullies, look your enemies in the eye and never retreat. Americans are supposed to work thirty hours a day, eight days a week; know what teamwork means; and rise from office boy to president. The United States of America expects you to be a hero, to stand up and be counted, to show the stuff you are made of.

I know the stuff I am made of: pipe-stem bones, an overbite and a long, tender nose. I have poor teeth, one slightly crossed eye, am tone deaf and have a pain threshold at the level of a firm handshake. I am constructed 180 degress out of phase with the pioneer spirit, the daring do, the raw courage and the adventurousness that made America great.

Since man is a totality, a physical psychological whole, I have other drawbacks. I jump at loud noises, and when younger perspired if a girl entered the room, and was known to vomit if sent to the principal's office. I found early on that standing up to bullies meant either a blow to the nose, sending me into a black pit of indescribable pain, or a shot to the mouth, leaving my upper lip full of teeth.

We are built, wrote physiologist Walter Cannon, for fight or flight. I was built for flight, and nature never intended me to do anything else. I fulfill the function of my particular structure by taking to my heels when trouble brews.

But what American boy would accept that, or what American parent? Is it possible that someone can find contact sports painful to the point of nausea, get faint at the prospect of tackling a runner in the open field and still be all any American can be—a hero to himself? The answer is yes.

Take my operation, for instance. A gallbladder operation is an elective, clean, soft-tissue operation involving only minor trauma. Mr. Average American with his high pain threshold usually can breeze through the hospitalization part of gallbladder surgery —the part I don't want to talk about or even remember. The pain of those few days was beyond my imagination. I never knew such agonies existed. While others were grumbling about being kept in the hospital, I was still struggling to get out of bed.

Where I finally triumphed was during my post-operative recovery. That's where being thin and bony came to mean something. That's where I outdistanced those muscular heroes who were packing their bags three days after leaving the operating room. That's where I found that physical cowards can handle pain —as long as it is self-inflicted. We can suffer and endure as long as the enemy is ourselves.

Ten days after my surgery, I started jogging. Less than three weeks after the surgery, I ran 35:01 in a five-mile race over very tough hills at Van Cortlandt Park. Within another month, I had brought that seven-minute-a-mile average down to 6:30 in a nine-mile race on the same course, my best time in three years.

Each race was as painful as any I can remember. The hills were almost unbearable. There were miles and miles of groans and gasps, interspersed with appeals to the Almighty. But that is something that happens almost every weekend in a runner's life. It is the kind of pain he can handle—and others can't.

Some muscular surgeons called my post-operative recovery "fantastic," but it was no odd or wonderful thing. It was just an ordinary accomplishment for thousands of distance runners who are constructed like I am. We would rather run twenty-six miles into a near-coma than be hit on the nose or even have someone threaten to hit us on the nose.

For runners, as for others, the first rule is to know that you are normal. To find this normal, you can use some rules suggested thirty years ago by anthropologist Earnest Hooten.

"The body," wrote Hooten, "will guide us most rapidly and unerringly to the mind and personality. Body structure affords the safest and most accessible takeoff for the exploration of individual personality."

Translated, this means that if you have a weak little body fit for running from fights and altercations, you should do so. Your body tells you who and what you are. If you listen well, you can be a success, perhaps a hero, even though no one else may be aware of it.

Just remember, function follows structure—and so does fulfillment.

"Know yourself."

What was written on the temple of Apollo, we must now write in even larger letters where we can see it every day. Know yourself, so you may live that life peculiar to you, the one and only life you were born to live. Know yourself, that you may perfect your body and find your play. Know yourself, that you are not only the patient but also the therapist. Know yourself, that you may accept that knowledge.

For the Greeks, the time for this discovery was leisure—a time that also included activities like health, self-expression, character formation, personality and self-adjustment. Included, of course, were play and the training of the body. We are, wrote Plato, playthings of the gods and life must be lived as play. The body, in Plato's opinion, was the source of all energy and initiative.

Therefore, we must know our body, its strengths, its weaknesses, its likes, its dislikes. Socrates stated that a sensible man should know what is good or bad for him better than any physician. And later, Tiberius said that anyone who had lived for twenty years should be able to take care of himself without a doctor.

We are, then, to become experts in ourselves. I should learn not from books or from others, but from my own experience. I should understand myself by self-study rather than by consulting the professional. The body is here to be seen. Visible, measurable, it delivers its message. Stripped down before a mirror, it reveals to me who I am.

Similarly, I can know my own temperament—that level of my personality where I express my desires and motivation and interact with other people. Here again, I am as circumscribed as I am in my body. I have a particular mixture of traits which I can change only in a very narrow range. Like me or not, I am what I am.

"My purpose," says sports psychologist William Beausay, "is to help the individual athlete improve performance through the knowledge of his own psychology and the way to get the most out of it."

That certainly sounds as if Professor Beausay is on the side of the angels. He is going to help us jocks "to know thyself" (Plato); "to be what thou art" (Nietzsche); "to be the self one truly is" (Kierkegaard).

The professor has tested middle linebackers and Indy 500 drivers, and has found them cut from the same cloth. They are nervous, depressed, dominant, hostile, aggressive and impulsive. They also perform beautifully. Beausay is nonjudgmental about these qualities. He is a pragmatist. The only way a line-backer can improve his dominance, hostility and aggressiveness is to be more dominant and hostile and aggressive. Beausay shows them how.

It is only when he turns to distance runners that he reveals his failure to grasp the true role of psychology. Distance runners, he reports, score surprisingly low in hostility and dominance. "Most runners," he states, "seem to be passive, submissive followers." But instead of developing these traits and making distance runners more of what they are, as he has the football players and race-car drivers, he would change them. He would give them the psychic attitude of the Indy drivers. "When that happens," he says, "the world mile record will come down a full 10 seconds."

I am sure that Professor Beausay believes this to be progress. Distance runners just have no business, he thinks, being tolerant and submissive. And so we are faced with the age-old problem where men of conviction, either religious or scientific, would populate the world with people who fit their idea of what is good or normal or successful.

Making runners hostile and aggressive (or football players passive and tolerant) is unnatural and completely counter to their temperament and personality. It is bound to fail. It would be easier to make a rabbit a killer. Unfortunately, this self-evident truth has escaped psychologist Beausay and indeed most of the scientific community. Its members continue to ply us with books explaining man as if he were some homogenous composition of traits and values instead of the infinite variety he is.

In the past this sort of thinking insisted on a single way to theological salvation. Now, it insists on a single way to social salvation. Beausay would have runners turn hostile and aggressive to break world records. Harvard Professor Richard Herrnstein would have them be hostile and aggressive to save our social structure.

Society, according to Herrnstein, thrives on our socio-economic competition. Should our disparities in wealth and status be eliminated we would, he predicts, have prompt social and economic disaster.

We distance runners certainly don't want Dr. Herrnstein's and our society to fail for want of aggressive, dominant, confident, adventurous and courageous men (and I'm sure it won't), but we shouldn't be expected to change our behavior to suit anyone's theory. And all those who delight in large family gatherings and love an evening at the theater should not be offended if we would rather spend those hours with a good book or on a solitary run.

We runners are not built for the rat race or the community of men. Turning distance runners who are made for flight and thought into fighters or socializers goes against nature.

Near the end of my hour's run on the river road is a long, steep hill. On certain days I see it in the distance, and remember its length and height and slope. Then, I think of the effort it will take and how I will feel at the top, and I wish I were already back in town, the run over, doing other things.

On those days, my mind is in command. I am a

reasoning, calculating human being. I have forgotten I am also my body and that my body accepts such challenges. My body wants to be stretched as far as it can go and then stretched even further. I have forgotten that the body wants the best and the true just as much as my mind and heart do. It will not be satisfied until it has reached its limits. On those days, I am not a runner. I am a mind.

On other days, I gratefully accept the challenge. I run at the hill with all my might. I spend ninety seconds or more at flank speed with all systems at go. I let my body take control. Once having willed the action, I am content to receive the messages from the feet and legs and thighs, to hear from the heart and lungs and brain, to listen to why my body tells me, to listen but not to interfere.

It has taken years to reach this stage, to become a listener, to learn from my body and teach myself not to inflict my ignorance on it, to allow my body to seek its own perfection.

It takes that long to learn the craft, develop the technique, submit to the discipline. "What tedious training, day after day, year after year, never ending," wrote Emerson, "to form common sense." But after tedium comes enlightenment. Where the unaided intellect fails, the body now reveals. As I race up that hill, I am a pupil, an observer. My body is my tutor.

It is, after all, the finite body, my imperfect body, which is trying to express the infinite my soul would have me be. And it is the finite body which is the first to tell me who I am. Therefore, the mind's first step to self-awareness must be through the body.

"Who is one truly," asked Abraham Maslow, "if not first one's own body, one's own constitution, one's own functioning?" And how else is this to be learned but by hearing those inner signals, those directives from within, the voice of the real self?

In that long, painful surge as I attack that hill, I experience those signals, those directives, those voices. Now, instinct is in command, not reason. I am listening to a body which has taken complete control. On those days, I am not a runner. I am my body.

For a good part of my day, I am no more than a robot. My actions are pure reflex. My body is on automatic pilot. It is programmed to take care of the demands of my outer world while I escape to my inner one. For the better part of my time, I am like a captain who has given control of the ship to a junior officer and retired to his cabin to read his favorite author. I have made routine things in my day so routine that they get done without me being aware I am doing them. Unfortunately, things also don't get done, or are done badly, or done in the wrong place at the wrong time.

Some would say that this inattention to the ordinary requirements for maintenance and survival is due to my upbringing. It is true that I was spoiled by my parents. I have, in fact, never had to take care of myself. I went through my entire education, including college and medical school, without leaving home. Then, there was the Navy and officer quarters, and finally marriage.

I am, therefore, in terms of ability to survive, still an

infant. My natural habitat is in someone's protective arms. I suspect, however, that even if I had taken to backpacking and become a mountain man, I would still be plagued by the effects of this retreat into the mind. I would right now be standing somewhere wondering how in the world I had gotten there and where in the world were those vital paraphernalia I had in my possession just a moment ago.

Whatever the reason, nature or nurture, my waking time is filled with excursions into the recesses of my mind. In the outer world, I am a reluctant citizen. I am continually breaking laws, both physical and social. When I am with my dear, dead friends in my head, I often pass my live ones with glazed eyes and not a sign of recognition.

My family has grown accustomed to this. My absentmindedness is now part of our tradition. I am expected to forget errands and birthdays and phone messages and the like. It causes no comment when I have no money for gas, or the restaurant bill, or the turnpike tolls. They are not surprised when I forget the names of their friends or even their own. They are not upset when I ask them to repeat a question. Hence, I am given only the simplest of tasks, the minimum of responsibilities. My family has arranged for life to go on, not without me but around me.

This works well until I get away from home. Away from home, I am a disaster. Every attempt, of course, is made to minimize what is in any case inevitable. I am sent off with a manilla envelope containing flight number and destination and the names of who will pick me up and who will deliver me, with all the correspondence about the meeting and the program which I had been meaning to read but never got around to. It also contains an absolutely essential piece of information—the title of my speech. As I enter my car, I am a sixty-year-old version of the first-grader going to school with a note pinned to his jacket.

The manilla folder works no better than the note. Before I sit down to read it, I must first get to the airport. That becomes a problem when I am leaving from Kennedy or LaGuardia because my body always drives to Newark. Having gotten to the correct airport and the right airline after another wrong turn or two, I may have to return to the car in the parking lot for my ticket, wallet or glasses, or all three.

One weekend, I went to Indianapolis with a physician friend from South Africa who is thirty years my junior. We were to do a sports medical clinic, and then go to Muncie to visit Dr. David Costill and his wife, Judy. By the time we reached Indianapolis, he had begun to assess the situation.

"George," he said, "from now on, I will be in charge of the tickets."

That took care of the tickets, but when we unpacked at the Costills' I was already missing my glasses and one yellow sock. By nightfall, I could not find a T-shirt I had received as part of the clinic and also the *Runner's World* shirt I had lectured in. Something odd was happening and I began to wonder about the Costill house. I was reminded of a home I stayed in at Crowley, Louisiana. When I reported a shoe missing at breakfast, I was told I would never find it. "This house," my hostess said, "eats things."

In the morning, I discovered it was me, not the house. The shirts were in a drawer. I had broken the basic rules of ineffectual losers on the road: One, do not unpack; and two, if you do, under no circumstances put things in drawers or hang them behind the door in the bathroom. Otherwise, instead of bringing home a memento, you will leave one.

Then, the glasses fell out of the shirt, so I was in good shape except for the yellow sock. I told Judy Costill about it as we left for a ten-mile run.

It was a tough ten. No relfex here. I went to the lead and resisted any attempt to pass me. I was no longer reading in the cabin; I was at the helm. I was in charge. This was the type of survival that claimed my full attention, the kind of maintenance worth my total participation. I was in touch with myself and everything around me in that bright early-morning sunshine.

We came into the final quarter of a mile, running abreast now, still flat-out but feeling good. The gym came into sight and then a tiny cluster of people at the finish point. Right in the middle was Dave Costill, waving what appeared to be a victory flag. As I got closer, I could see what it was: a last-minute behind-the-bathroom-door find by Judy Costill—my pajama pants.

The yellow sock? It was in one of the shoes I had worn while speaking in Indianapolis. I found it when I got home.

2

The Fitness

We are born with a seventy-year warranty. Some of us, for genetic reasons, are slated for significantly longer lifespans. In any case, it would appear that this longevity quotient is predetermined. So why exercise? It is not going to change our life expectancy. It is time-consuming and frequently boring. It is, in a word, a bother. So why bother?

There are, it seems to me, a variety of reasons. Exercise may not lengthen our lifespan, but it will certainly combat the problems that are said to shorten it: hypertension, obesity, addiction to nicotine, high cholesterol. What we are coming to know is that the insurance against these risk factors is almost always diet plus exercise.

Dr. Ralph Parffenberger has reported evidence that 2,000 calories a week spent on some sweaty activity will significantly lower the risk of coronary artery disease. Weight loss, salt restriction and exercise are also the primary ways to control hypertension. Similarly, most drug-dependent diabetics can stop medication with weight loss, exercise and a complex-carbohydrate diet.

Exercise, therefore, takes you a long way toward realizing your total longevity quotient. In addition to its effects on such measurable things as weight, pulse, blood pressure, blood sugar and cholesterol, exercise has a psychologically beneficial effect on the desire for cigarettes and food. It substitutes a positive addiction that tends to build the body for a negative one that tears the body down.

But if you talk about life expectancy being altered by exercise, you can still get an argument. There is just not enough evidence to satisfy the scientist—enough, perhaps, for practitioners who mix art with science in treating patients, but not enough for those who understand statistics, programs and the necessity for conclusive experiments. Proof positive is still lacking.

If, however, by "life expectancy" you mean *what you expect out of life today,* there is no contest. Anyone who exercises regularly can attest to their increase in energy. In addition, there are physical and psychological changes that enable us to life life in full, to live at the peak of our powers.

That should be our aim: to live each day totally; to live it, as Marcus Aurelius said, as if it were to be our last.

Exercise, particularly exercise that is play, allows us

to do that. Not only does it enable us to become totally fit, but it is accomplished in a playful activity which we would be willing to do on the day we die.

When exercise becomes play, it becomes a self-renewing compulsion. It becomes part of each day, part of your life. The fitness that ensues is simply a bonus. In fact, if fitness remains the primary purpose and the play is never discovered, in all likelihood the fitness program will fail. Only people with the proverbial gun in their ribs will persist. Only those under doctor's orders—because of a prior heart attack or some disease requiring exercise—will persevere in an activity that they find boring, mindless and time-consuming.

Play, of course, is quite the opposite. It occupies us totally, and time passes without our noticing it. Play is one of those peak experiences described by Abraham Maslow. It is the priceless ingredient in exercise. We should be like children at play.

Suppose you accept this thesis, acknowledge the need to play and the benefits of the exercise that comes with it. How would you find your play?

First, you must discover what you do best, which means analyzing your body structure. Function follows structure, so the body usually reveals how it functions best.

Having done that, you must analyze your temperament to see how you like to play. Are you built for flight, fight or negotiation? Is your tendency under stress to withdraw, to socialize or to become aggressive? Is your nature predisposed to detachment, dependence or dominance?

All of us have a little of each tendency in us, but one force is dominant and usually decides whether we prefer to play sports as a loner, or part of a highly social activity, or want to go head-to-head physically with an opponent. Fortunately, our structure usually goes along with these choices.

The solitary individual usually is thin-boned, stringy-muscled and equipped for endurance sports. He finds running an intensely satisfying exercise-play which indeed can become part of his life style.

The socializers may not be natural athletes. If their bodies possess neither strength nor endurance, they can still enjoy sports like golf, doubles tennis, cycling, skiing, skating and running. They are particularly good at aquatic sports. But the primary and engrossing part of their play-exercise is other people.

The hitters, on the other hand, need other people not as companions but as opponents. They play the big game in tennis, tend to increase the suspense in golf by betting and often become engaged in activities such as the martial arts, weight lifting and hitting the heavy bag.

Having begun with the question, "Why exercise?" we find that the answer is to be found in yet another question: "Why *play*?"

When we begin an exercise program, it is almost always for the wrong reasons. We seek physical fitness because we believe we *have* our bodies and want to do something to them, not because we *are* our bodies and wish to find out who we are.

It is an understandable error. Historically, society —the church, the school, the corporation—has taught us an abnormal view of the body. The preachers have warned us against the excesses of the flesh; that the body is an instrument of the devil, something to be disciplined and denied. The intellectuals have taught us that the body is a mere conveyance, a mundane vessel for the triumphs of the mind. Keep the body in repair and it won't bother our essential function, which is thinking. And what of businessmen? They have perceived the body as a machine, a tool. Fitness makes us better workers, improves our output.

The body, then, has been treated as a second-class citizen. Anyone who would think otherwise must develop his own rules, come to a different view of the universe. He must question what he hears from the pulpit, wonder how his childhood teachers could miss the point, and look on the laws of supply and demand as necessary only for the preservation of the herd. He must somehow discover that his body is equal with his soul.

Oddly enough, this unity occurs most readily in play and sports, and in those exercise programs where the magical and the mystical have taken over from the practical and the pragmatic. We should know, as Ortega said, that life demands two different kinds of effort—one stemming from sheer delight, originality, creativity, vitality, spontaneity; the other effort ruled by compulsion, obligation, utility. The former is sport, the most important part of life. The latter, work or labor, ranks second.

Ortega concludes, "Life . . . resides in the first alone; the rest is relatively mechanical and functioning."

The millions who get into exercise programs will succeed or fail, therefore, inasmuch as they move beyond the details of fitness—beyond tables and charts and schedules—and into the vital, creative area of play. Beyond fitness itself, everyone is a child—a child at play but also a child, as Blake said, grown wise.

The truth is that play is where we live. In running and climbing and swimming, in hunting and fishing, in riding horses and playing games we become ourselves and open ourselves to experience. There, we find an inward calm and peace. There, thinking and feeling have a clarity that occurs almost nowhere else. And there, we discover a wholeness, a completion and an integrity that makes us want to celebrate our being. Away from daily life, away from politics and religion, from economics and science, we see the universe and ourselves as being much more than logic and reason have taught us.

Exercise to lose weight. Run to lower your blood pressure. Bicycle to reduce your cholesterol. Swim to increase your cardiac function. Play tennis to help your breathing. Golf so you'll sell more clients. Do calisthenics to clear your brain. All those things are good. But beyond all this fitness is the discovery of who you are.

The written word must be suspect. If you are denied truth firsthand, however, make sure the truth you get is no worse than secondhand. If you are going to rely on an expert, let him speak directly to you and not through someone else. If you read about something outside of your experience, be sure you read the original and not the commentary.

One instance where the commentary missed the truth of the original was the press treatment of an article on running that appeared in *Physician and Sportsmedicine.* Written by Dr. William Morgan, a psychologist, the article was titled, "Negative Addiction in Runners." That title, which conveys less than half the story, caught the attention of the press. What followed was a nationwide warning about the dangers of running.

The *Chicago Tribune,* for example, led off its review of the Morgan report in this fashion: "A growing number of joggers and runners are becoming so addicted to their foot-pounding pursuits that they are developing the same kind of problem as heroin users."

After this opening came a litany of the disorders caused by the search for a running "fix," as well as a list of withdrawal symptoms which occur when these addicts are unable to run.

But as I read the original research report on what the newspapers would have me believe is self-destruction, I saw only the positive aspects of running. By the time I had finished reading "Negative Addiction in Runners," I was convinced that running is a *positive* not a negative addiction. Reading between the lines, I perceived running as an affirmative discovery of the self.

Morgan, you must understand, was not out to condemn running. His previous research had convinced him of the beneficial effects of exercise, especially on depression. All of his earlier studies had been positive. This treatise was simply about runners who tended, in his opinion, to carry running a bit too far. But then, we always have been aware of this tendency. Man is a maximizer, ripe for excesses and exuberances. When life becomes a celebration, we are likely to over-celebrate.

Let's look more closely at what Morgan has to say before forming a judgment.

"I would like to suggest that running be viewed as a wonder drug." Morgan takes his stand immediately. Running is good for you. It is one of the great scientific breakthroughs of the century. It can be a panacea not only for the body but for the mind as well. But as with all therapy, you must tailor the dose, beware of abuses, avoid the bad reaction. Then, running not only restores your health; it adds to it.

"Exercise makes people feel good. No wonder they get addicted to it." That is, of course, the addiction we need—a positive one, a self-renewing compulsion to do what is good for us. The difference between running and drugs is the absence of fantasy. The good feeling in and from running is no delusion. It is an accurate perception of what is actually taking place in our whole being—body, mind and spirit.

"We begin running just to stay in shape, but soon we are seduced by the sense of clarity, energy and self-esteem accompanying the daily run." This is the good news. A true clarity, energy and self-esteem, not a false one, is available to us out on the roads. What we are seduced by are the negative addictions which destroy our bodies, and our minds and souls with them. Running is a purifying discipline.

"The running experience should not become an end in itself, because at this point runners may lose perspective, internalize questionable priority systems and place self above everything else." Runners, of course, see it differently. Running is an end in itself, as well as a means. It does change our perspective. It does give us the sense of humor to see ourselves as we never have before. And it does drive us to adjust our priorities toward our own truths and rules and roles, not those thrust upon us.

We do move inwardly, but only so we can later move outwardly toward union with others; so that the self we destroy is the false one we have been carrying all these years, the one that is no longer necessary.

Thoreau went into the woods because he feared that when he came to die he would discover that he had not lived. He wanted to life deeply and suck the marrow out of life. Each of us has the same fear, the same desire. And we also know there are experiences that are, as Thoreau said, "indescribable, infinite, all-absorbing, divine, heavenly pleasure."

But Thoreau also wrote, "I looked to books for some recognition of kindred experience, but strange to say I found none."

The printed word rarely matches the experience.

"Exercise addicts," wrote William Morgan, "give higher priority to their daily runs than job, family and friends. They run first, and then if time permits they work, love and socialize."

But surely that is the correct sequence. First come fitness and play, energy and self-discovery. We must first be made whole. Then, we can return to the busy world of affairs. We must first go back to being a child before we can do those adult things.

Still, the runner's attention to self bothers Morgan. "As the runner becomes more aware of the self," he warns, "there is less interest in vocational achievement."

The key word here is "vocation." What indeed is my calling? And if I am responding to that call, am I capable of meeting the demands it makes?

Chances are, the runner's search for self will also reveal which work will be a witness to that self. The chances also are that running will lead to true achievement in whatever that field is. It will, if nothing else, lead to looking at all day-to-day activities from a new point of view.

"Genius," said William James, "is just another way of looking at things." Running develops our particular and peculiar genius, and gives us the audacity to put that vision into action.

When Bill Rodgers was teaching school, he ran during most of his free time. One day, the principal called him into the office. "Bill," he told him, "you will have to make a decision. The time has come to concentrate on your vocation." Rodgers took his advice. He quit teaching. He had arrived at a point described by Morgan:

> Monetary rewards become irrelevant to the exercise addict, who has moved in an inward direction, become quiescent, at terms with his environment, at peace with himself. Such a point of view may not only limit professional growth, but it can actually jeopardize one's employment.

But personal growth must precede professional growth. What you do in your profession is a function of the person you are. That must, therefore, be your top priority.

What is personal growth? I like something Robert Frost wrote in his account of an all-star baseball game. What those athletes demonstrated, he said, were the four attributes needed for any achievement: prowess, courage, justice and knowledge.

Running is my means to those ends. Training gives me the prowess, the race gives me courage. And then I begin to see what justice means—being true first to myself, extracting every ounce out of every talent I possess, and then being true to others and to my profession. I know that job, family, friends will wait while I run. In fact, they must await the outcome of my runs. And that outcome depends upon the lifetime that is in every day of running.

So there it is. Can anything have a higher priority than running? It defines me, adds to me, makes me whole. I have a job and family and friends who can attest to that.

It was inevitable that we would see articles in the magazines and the press taking a negative view on running. The pendulum always swings. Each action provokes a reaction: The "outs" become the "ins," the rebels become the Establishment, ripe for attack.

In the beginning, when running was first catching on, the press was filled with enthusiastic articles extolling the virtues of the sport. Journalists are sensitive to enthusiasm. They have antennae that pick up any electricity being generated in the community. They could sense a new idea developing, so they made running the darling of the media.

But every enthusiasm provokes an inescapable backlash. Innovation which generates sympathy becomes orthodoxy which stimulates criticism. The sport for the lonely long-distance runner became the sport of the masses. It became fair game, and also interesting reading to knock its hat off.

The journalists at both ends of this process, and also those who read them, miss the point. Running, which was originally praised for the wrong reasons is now damned for shortcomings most runners would see as only incidental problems.

Journalists, you see, are much like trial lawyers. They are forced to become instant experts in the subject at hand. They aquire masses of information. Then, they have to digest this data and process it into readable prose. The end result is the map, not the territory. It is the menu, not the meal. It is truth secondhand.

We will never discover truth secondhand. If I am to write the truth or know it when I read it, I must first live it. I must touch it, taste it, smell it and hear it. I have to sense it, become aware of it, give it my unmixed attention.

We cannot delegate that instruction to anyone else —not to the journalists, not even to the experts. I cannot understand something I have not gone through myself. I must live my own causes and then experience my own effects. This is a never-ending, ever-changing process. Whatever conclusion I come to today, I will undoubtedly modify tomorrow. I can never make the absolute statement.

Journalists, like trial lawyers, want none of that. They want to simplify, not amplify. They want yes-and-no answers. They are looking for the nonexistent final and definitive word on the subject. So, no matter how sincere, how open, how willing to present both sides, the journalists are bound to fail. They truly do need "inside" information.

I had a reporter call me for help in writing an article about running a marathon. While talking to him I realized it was an absurd situation. I should have been writing the article, not him. Eventually, he would have to edit my words, then filter my experience through his own experience, and he could not do that.

Knowledge, the philosophers say, is a function of being. There has to be a change in the being of the knower for there to be a change in the nature and amount of knowing.

Emerson said it plain: "What we are, that only we can perceive."

If I wish to understand running and runners, I must first become a runner myself. I must go through at least the minimum of the sensations and the excitements and the fulfillments of the runner's life. I must live with some program involving effort and discipline, fatigue and pain. I must experience the "feel" of running.

How, then, can we evaluate critical articles on running, or indeed on any human activity? Most important is to be sure the writer is writing from inside the subject rather than outside.

3

The Cures

A friend in Dallas gave me a watch. I had gone without one for more than a decade and had done nicely. I had handled my day without a watch and felt no need for one. I had, in fact, lost my watch while raking leaves one day and had not raked leaves or worn a watch since. I believe, you see, in signs.

Nevertheless, I took the new watch. He is a good friend and was quite insistent. He actually took it off his wrist and put it on mine. So I let it stay. Besides, it is a marvelous instrument—one of those modern-day wonders of miniaturization and circuitry. It not only tells time; it is a stopwatch that can give me lap times as well. Further, it has an alarm to warn me, for instance, when my time is up during a speech. It also gives the date.

When he gave me the watch, I told him I could see

the value of all its functions except the date. When I run, I do not have a clock in my head. I usually have no idea what time I am doing, so a stopwatch can come in handy during a race or in training. And I do have a habit of speaking too long. It is not often a man my age with a large family gets a chance to speak for any length of time without interruption. Once I begin to interact with an audience, I forget time and need something or someone to bring me back to reality.

But the date—who needs that? Why all these additional elements in the watch just to tell me the date? The date, it seemed to me, was overkill. This Japanese watch had one capability too many, one function that was unnecessary.

"Irving," I said to my friend, "one thing I do know is the date."

Now, I don't know the date. The watch knows the date. I am a victim of what I have come to call the "Japanese Watch Syndrome." I have allowed technology to come between me and my perception of the world.

I can operate without knowing the date. It is, in fact, a desired state for anyone who wants to be a child, an athlete or a saint. Knowing the date more often than not indicates a preoccupation with the past or future that is hostile to genuine living. Knowing the date is rarely accompanied by feelings of joy.

When I am concentrating on the date, the odds are that I am concentrating on nothing else that is important. Chances are, I am missing out on those experiences which occur only when I am in a timeless state where past and present and future come together.

I would like, however, when I finally come back to reality after those mystical moments, to have some idea of what day of the week it is and even what month without referring to that infernal watch. My aim in this life is to be as independent as possible. The watch continually reminds me of failure. I am, if anything, becoming more dependent and must fight this tendency every day.

If you look, you can see this dependency all around you. The machine (or the expert behind the machine) monitors our acts, replaces our instincts, substitutes for our intuitions, acts as judge for our insights. The machine tells us what to do. In the process, our instincts are no longer heard. The animal in us is caught and caged, and no longer has to live on the alert.

Our best course demands exactly the opposite. If I am to be a good animal, I must live on the alert. I must develop my instincts. I must be able to hear and interpret what goes on in my body. I cannot be a blind and deaf tenant of my body. I cannot relax and sit back without sacrificing yet another function and capability of my body to technology.

Technology must be seen for what it is—both good and bad. It frees us, certainly. It liberates us from work that is drudgery. It shortens the work week. It transforms society and gives us leisure which is simply, as the Greeks knew, a school for becoming oneself.

At the same time, technology has removed physical stress, atrophied our legs and bodies, and allowed us to gain weight as only affluent societies do. It has taken over the decision-making process in our day-today living. Computers now tell us what to eat, how to sleep, what shoes to wear, how hard and how long to exercise. We merely establish what we want done, and the experts can program us for it. No need to use, for instance, our inborn power to perceive exertion; they will do that for us with a treadmill. No need to trust the signals we are getting from our body; they will run a printout of eighteen tests which will tell us exactly how we feel.

When this happens to me, I become no more than a guided missile, my life's trajectory already plotted out. I lose the chance to be me. I am now ruled by clocks, calendars, schedules, agendas; living in an environment that is self-correcting and almost void of physical stress.

Abraham Maslow spoke of "subjective biology" or "experiential biology" where we are aware of the inner signals in the body. He saw the great need to hear these "voices of the real self," to know what and whom one likes and dislikes, what is enjoyable and what is not, when to eat and when not to, when to sleep, when to urinate, when to rest.

My Japanese watch is a symbol. I may not have a real need to know the date, but there is no question that I no longer know it. Technology can do that. Our task is to use technology without being enslaved by it. It must help us become more human rather than less.

It was Williams James who spoke of saints as being athletic, and athletes being "secular saints." For James, who was a constant seeker after man's potential, the coexistence of bodily and spiritual perfection was not a coincidence.

This theme—that saints are athletic and that athletes are, in some measure, saintly and that the common man can aspire to be both—never received the attention it deserved. Theologians viewed sin rather than sainthood as the normal state of man. Physicians, preoccupied with disease, considered the athlete a physiological freak.

But times are changing. Both professions are becoming as interested in the here and now as in the hereafter, and are investigating man's capabilities for good rather than analyzing his faults and diseases. For the physicians, this means the emergence of sports medicine as a new and major specialty.

A result of this work is the *Encyclopedia of Sports Medicine*. It runs to 1,707 pages and is culled from just about as many manuscripts, filled with fact and unfortunately a great deal of speculation.

"Probably 50 percent of the topics," said the editor, the late Albert Hyman, "lack solid research data." Such refreshing honesty doesn't obscure the fact that what is contained shakes many long-held theories in medicine.

One of these is the danger that athletics, if taken in large amounts, can lead to the development of the dreaded "athletic heart." The "athletic heart" describes a condition in which the heart muscle enlarges beyond the capacity of the heart's arteries to sustain it. This condition, according to Oklahoma City physician Dr. Dale Groom, does not exist, and he has the Tarahumara Indians to prove it.

For the Tarahumara, who lives in northern Mexico, running is the principal sport. It is at the same time his livelihood, his recreation and his criterion for success, since he hunts a deer by the simple method of running after it relentlessly for a couple of days until the animal drops from exhaustion. He also catches wild turkeys by pursuing them until they can no longer rise from the ground in flight.

But at play, the Tarahumara performs even more prodigious feats. His "kickball games," played by teams of men kicking a wooden ball about the size of a tennis ball, extend for distances up to 150 miles. This is no relay; each man runs the route.

The Indians examined by Groom ranged in weight from 114 to 135 pounds and were between five feet, two inches and five feet, six inches tall. They were all lean and fit (what else?), having almost no perceptible body fat. But most important was the finding that all these men with a lifetime of prodigious endurance activity had normal-sized hearts on X-rays, and normal electrocardiograms as well. On questioning the Indians, Groom could find no instance where anyone had dropped dead or became fatally ill from any of these almost interminable running sessions.

"Obviously, more questions than answers have been raised by this work," writes Groom. Where, for instance, do the Tarahumaras get the 11,000 calories needed for such a long race? Physiologists had already established that this is beyond the limit that can be expended by the body in a twenty-four-hour period. Have the Tarahumaras, asks Groom, received a special dispensation from some of the human limitations known to us?

If they have, I suspect it is because these limitations are artificial. They have been based upon our imperfect knowledge of what man can and cannot do.

"The phenomenal feats of these primitive Indians," concludes Dr. Groom, "afford convincing evidence that most of us brought up in this sedentary, comfortable civilization of today actually develop and use only a fraction of our cardiac reserve."

We are now coming full circle. Man, who originally lived or died on the basis of his bodily skills, is faced with this same predicament again. His life expectancy —living each day at the top of his powers rather than longevity—depends on getting the utmost out of his body.

Like most runners, I have become an endurance animal. I have attained the body composition, the cardiopulmonary function and the internal economy one would expect of an animal in the wild. I have reached training levels far beyond those needed for our current culture and have developed the body to match.

Looking at me, you would hardly suspect this. I look no different from most nice, ordinary, sedentary people you see every day. It is only when I go for a physical examination and have laboratory tests done that it becomes clear I am very different—or very sick. Almost every test done on me shows changes indicative of a disease state.

Since I am no different from thousands and thousands of other runners, the annual physical has become the annual fiasco. The animal is hardly back in its habitat when the phone rings and the doctor suggests some more tests or a short stay in the hospital.

One fifty-eight-year-old runner from Maine, who was averaging fifty miles a week, had not missed a day's work in years and felt like a young colt, was told he had the liver and kidneys of a seventy-year-old alcoholic.

Conditioning, you see, changes "normal" values. When we train, we can no longer use the standards established for spectators. There are laboratory findings that tell us we have gotten the most out of our bodies and give numbers that go with excellence. Unfortunately, these are also in many instances the same changes that doctors associate with disease. So we runners are told we are ill or about to become ill.

The truth is, of course, exactly the opposite. Dr. Joan Ullyot once told me she could predict how a runner would do in a marathon by the tests. If they were normal, she was sure the runner would do poorly. I feel the same. Whenever my blood tests are normal, I figure I'm not training hard enough.

What are these tests that confuse the doctor and frustrate the patient?

• *Blood count:* The blood count of the distance runner frequently shows a low hematocrit (39–42) and a low hemoglobin (12.5–14). Does this mean anemia? Not at all. In fact, the runner has more circulating hemoglobin mass than his inactive physician. There is, however, an even greater increase in blood volume, so the blood is slightly diluted.

• *Urine:* Runners frequently have blood cells and protein in their urine. This is normal and will clear in three to five days if the doctor can think of any way to get the runner to stop running that long.

• *Bold urea nitrogen (BUN):* Although this is usually elevated in runners, it does not indicate kidney disease. There is simply an increased turnover of waste products, and the kidney does not quite keep up.

• *Liver enzymes (SGPT):* These are elevated as much as two to three times normal. These levels do not mean liver disease, and will come back to normal if and when the running is stopped.

• *Heart enzymes (CPK):* Again, these enzymes may reach very high levels and are not indicative of any heart damage or disease.

• *Muscle enzymes (LDH):* As would be expected, these can rise to quite high levels with heavy training. Again, they are of no clinical significance.

(The tremendous elevation of heart and muscle enzymes, often occurring simultaneously, is alarming to the physician. Doctors find it difficult to conceive that a running program could result in such profound alterations of these tests. For this reason, runners are cautioned on the need for further study of the heart, liver or kidneys. All of the tests are, of course, unnecessary.)

• *Cholesterol:* Here, the runner is told of a negative change. The cholesterol level remains the same;

therefore, it is said, the running isn't doing any good. In fact, the good thing that is happening is in the ratio between "good" cholesterol (high-density lipids) and "bad" cholesterol (low-density lipids). HDL protects against coronary disease and is invariably elevated in an adequate running program. Total cholesterol correlates better with weight loss than fitness.

• *Bilirubin:* An elevated bilirubin is almost always present in distance runners. It is probably due to breakdown of red cells in the body. Again, it is not a sign of liver or blood disease, just part of the normal physiological changes with high mileage.

• *Uric acid:* This is a test that gets better when you run. Heavy-mileage runners lower their uric acid levels rather than raise them.

• *Enlarged heart:* The endurance animal has a larger heart than the animal that is domesticated or in captivity. The same thing happens with athletes. The largest hearts are found in professional cyclists, cross-country skiers and distance runners. This is a physiological response to training, the development of a capacious filling-type heart that can drive gallons of blood through the circulatory system. Spectators have little, shriveled-up hearts.

There are dozens of interesting ways in which the athlete differs from the spectator. This new breed of animal needs a new breed of doctor to examine him.

Most diseases are self-limited. If left to their own devices, most bodily ills will take their departure within forty days—if not sooner. Unless agitated by treatments and medicines, they have a natural life-expectancy of three to six weeks.

In the days before wonder drugs, this was part of our conventional wisdom. It was the consensus of the ancients, certainly, that we should treat disease with respect and not try to fight it. When fought, an illness was more likely to stand its ground and last a good deal longer.

Mark Twain had a unique response to sickness. It was his custom when ill to give up smoking and drinking and swearing. Soon afterward, the disease would become discouraged and go away.

You can read similar advice in Plato and Plutarch, in Galen and Montaigne. They way to go is the Twain way. Just hunker down and wait it out. Diet and rest, climate and light activity were the prescriptions of Hippocrates. Only when they failed would he wheel up the heavy artillery of drugs and surgery.

We should not regard this information as trivia. Neither drugs nor surgery will hasten the convalescence of most illnesses. Despite the wonder drugs, it still takes six weeks for a fracture to heal, to recover from a heart attack or go through a bout of rheumatic fever. It still takes, and always will, six weeks to recover to your preoperative work tolerance after major surgery.

What the natural history of disease tells us is to be patient. There is no sense rushing. We are lifelong athletes. Whatever seems of paramount importance today must always be evaluated from that very long-range view. There will be plenty of time to enjoy our sport and improve our performance. There is always another race.

Hippocrates said it all: "Life is short and art long; the crisis fleeting, experience perilous and decision difficult."

The impatient patient only makes it harder.

There is a healthy way to be ill, a healthy way to deal with disease, a healthy way to live with a sickness.

There is an old saying that the way to live a long life is to get a chronic disease and take care of it. It is simply a matter of following the golden rules of health, and making the effort to tap those energies and capabilities we have left untouched. There is no reason to take an illness lying down. Strength, stamina and vigor are still there for those willing to work for them.

To understand this, we must see the difference between disease and illness, and between curing and healing. A disease is a biologic event. It is an interaction of a pathologic process with our cells and organs. The curing of the disease is the removing, reversing or retarding of this process. Curing is the science of medicine.

Illness, on the other hand, is a *human* event. It is my reaction to my disease. Healing is the decreasing of my symptoms and the enhancing of my sense of physical and psychological well-being. Healing is the *art* of medicine.

Illness, then, is the way I perceive, experience and cope with disease. I have two choices: to delegate authority for its management or to accept it myself. I can watch the doctor or assume command; see the doctor as the all-knowing doer or as a teacher and companion in this cooperative venture—health.

Health, as I see it, cannot be conferred; it must be earned. I must make a personal decision. I must do more than wish or want health; I must *will* it. I must take the responsibility.

Both doctors and patients find this move toward the personal in medicine a difficult one. Patients are sometimes incredibly passive. My father once told me a story about a patient he had examined who then asked him, "How do I feel today, Doctor?"

Even more absurd is the doctor who isn't interested in how his patient feels. He treats lab tests, electrocardiograms and computer writeouts rather than a living, breathing, frightened, depressed human being. The physician who feels guilty when his science doesn't work must realize that the real enemy, as one patient said, is not death but inhumanity.

Health is the reverse. It is an affirmation of humanity. It is the determination to follow Thoreau's dictum: "The whole duty of man may be expressed in one line—make yourself a perfect body." Health comes from that active determination of my life style that perfects me whether I am sick or handicapped or disabled.

I am not saying that all of this will affect the disease itself. Exercise may not give me an extra day of life. It will, however, give extra life to every day. If it doesn't improve my vital capacity, it will improve my capacity for everything vital.

Peguy, the French philosopher, said that we die of our entire life. We live of it, too. Everything we do is important, and even more when we are living with a disease. For then we especially need that background of sanity and serenity and good humor conferred on us by vigorous exercise.

Specialists intent on tests and pathology often fail to see this. They don't particularly like things that can't be measured, felt or put on a slide and examined under a microscope. They demand hard facts and proof of cure. Therefore, they miss the fact that the patients have healed themselves.

I place in evidence some reports:

• *Item:* Sixteen asthmatic children ages twelve to fourteen were given a vigorous exercise program for three months. Only a few were already participating in sports, yet fifteen out of the sixteen tolerated the program well. The results showed no gains in oxygen transport, and the authors of the report concluded that the exercise was "unlikely to have longterm benefits on underlying asthmatic disease."

I ask, can we measure the health residing in play?

• *Item:* In a Mayo Clinic study, eight men with coronary heart disease were put on a year-long exercise program. No changes were found in their coronary artery X-rays or their left heart function. All, however, had a decrease in pain, an increase in self-esteem, and a more positive attitude toward their work and their disability.

My comment: Exercise has to do with physiology, not disease; with health, not heart attacks. These men had become men again. They had been healed.

• *Item:* A thirty-seven-year-old man with a past history of polio, now paralyzed in both legs, was examined because of a slow pulse due to his physical training. His daily program included several hours of walking exercises on crutches, then one hour or more of swimming and gymnastics, followed by two hours of crawling on the beach! The disease was unaffected; there was no improvement in paralysis.

I say, how can we hope to measure this man or be his equal in living?

A reader who had returned to running marathons after a bout with cancer wrote, "There is nothing more certain than the defeat of the man who gives up." And, I might add, the victory of one who will not.

I was speaking at a meeting of heart specialists when the question was raised: "Is exercise the best treatment for coronary artery disease?" My answer was immediate, direct and unqualified. "There is only one treatment for coronary artery disease," I said. "Surgery."

Coronary artery disease is a narrowing of the arteries that carry the blood to the heart muscle. This obstruction is organic and fixed. It cannot be altered; it must be circumvented. Blood must be detoured around the blockage. That is precisely what coronary artery bypass surgery does.

This does not mean, however, that surgery should be used routinely. It should, in fact, be the last alternative the physician considers. The doctor's first rule has always been to treat the patient, not the disease. Without altering the coronary obstruction, the cardiologist can do much to diminish its impact on the patient's body and psyche. Without increasing the blood flow through those arteries, the doctor can remove most of the physical limitations and the emotional stresses this disease causes in a patient's life.

To do this the physician must employ a subject generally ignored in medical school, exercise physiology. The study of the effect of exercise on the body. The science of human performance. Exercise physiology teaches us the process of health just as pathology teaches us the process of disease. To minimize the effects of disease we maximize the benefits of health.

Physiology helps everyone sick or well to mobilize his total energies. "The plain fact remains," said William James, "that men the world over possess amounts of resources that only exceptional individuals push to their extreme use. We have a habit of inferiority to our full self. Compared to what we ought to be we are only half awake."

Fortunately, coronary disease does wake people up. It does motivate. It does make them receptive to the discipline that exercise physiology demands. The coronary patient is ready to accept a personal responsibility for health. To follow Emerson's rule, "Look not outside yourself for strength or truth."

The physician, once more the teacher, can now say, "This is your problem, not mine. This is what you must do, not what I will do for you." The patient must act, not be acted upon. The prescription is not drugs but effort; not medicine but exercise and diet and a change in attitude. And the best model the patient can use is the athlete.

The athlete model has the additional advantage of being familiar to all of us. Further, unlike most advice dispensed by physicians, athletic practices make sense. They should. They use the application of the best that is known in exercise physiology, the fruits of the research designed to get the most out of the human animal.

The first step is the process of getting into shape. Observing the athlete we learn that this is done quite slowly. The athlete goes to a training camp in order to be in peak condition when the season starts. So too with the coronary patient. At first the stress applied must be minimum, both in time and intensity and frequency. Then each factor is gradually increased.

The athlete also has to diet. The overweight athlete is a target for ridicule. Leanness is the most obvious characteristic of athletes, particularly of the distance runner. In fact, as a group they appear weak and undernourished, even haggard. There is good reason for this. The oxygen delivery system is based in part on our body weight. Each pound of body fat we lost increases our available oxygen 1 percent or more. A genuine weight loss where diet is accompanied by exercise can improve our efficiency enormously.

There are other athletic practices that are also instructive. Not eating before a race, for instance. So too the coronary patient. Effort should be done on an empty stomach. And then the warmup, essential to the heart patient.

The athlete learns to avoid smoking and curtail drinking; the heart patient learns much the same thing. And so it goes down the line. The more the life style of the coronary artery patient approximates that of the athlete the better.

Other good things are happening during this process. The personality changes for the better. Signs of the hurry sickness diminish. Attention to deadlines becomes less obsessive. Self esteem improves. The patient begins to feel more at home, more in control of what is happening from day to day.

These changes are generated by the maximally functioning athletic body. And that is necessary whether we have coronary artery disease or not. Life itself, as Beckett said, can be a terminal illness. We can go either way. Succumb to fear or anxiety or depression, retreat into a sedentary defensive existence. Or extend ourselves to our limitless limits and thereby make actual all that is potential.

Once motivated the execution of such a plan may be quite simple. Witness Kierkegaard's advice. "Above all, do not lose your desire to walk; every day I walk myself into a state of well being and walk away from every illness; I have walked myself into my best thoughts and I know of no thought so burdensome that I cannot walk away from it."

The cardiologists were waiting for a final word. "Before you begin to treat a patient's arteries be sure you have bypassed the patient's previous existence. Before you take the patient to surgery be sure you have taken the patient to the playing fields."

Only when becoming an athlete fails should we treat the disease itself.

I was cruising along the river road, locked in on automatic pilot, when disaster struck. Not all at once, of course; first there were some premonitory symptoms. It was not discomfort I would normally attend to, but then the back of the mid-thigh is not a place a distance runner usually has trouble.

I presumed it was nothing. But the nagging increased, and on the long downhill to the bridge just about six miles out, I thought of walking. Halfway across the bridge, the pain exploded into a searing sensation that brought me to a halt. I had to phone home and have someone come and get me.

My first reaction was fear. This had to be a very serious condition. Something dreadfal was evidently going on in that thigh muscle. I was initially immobilized by the pain, then I became immobilized by fear. Might I never be able to run again? Once a hamstring pull, the saying goes, always a hamstring pull.

In the next few hours, it became evident that this was indeed something that was going to last. It was not just a cramp. I could not tolerate any pressure on the back of my thigh. Even sitting down was painful. That night, I drove to New York and gave a clinic on sports medicine. As I answered the questions I had to limp from one side of the stage to the other. The doctor had become the patient.

I soon discovered that I was just like every other patient. I wanted help, I wanted it right now, and I was willing to try anything. I was suddenly at odds with the physician inside of me. For years, I had been dealing with runners and their injuries, answering their questions logically, rationally, pointing out the uselessness of drugs when the problem was the postural and structural imbalance of the body. These injuries, I had told telephone callers from as far away as Johannesburg, are not acts of God. They are due to the weakness or inflexibility of the muscles. No amount of boiling or baking or drugs or vitamins will help. You have to go back to basics and restructure the body.

But now I was the one in pain. I was the one hobbling around. And now I knew logic and reason are not enough. You can't trust a doctor, I told myself. Shaw said that every profession is a conspiracy against the laity. When you become a patient, you remember William James and his dictum, "Truth is what works."

Was there a chance the whirlpool would work? I was in it. How about ultrasound? Lay it on me. Would Butazolidine help? Give me a handful. What about vitamins? You never know. I was there taking them by the hour—first the C, then the B, then the rest of the alphabet.

A week before, I had received a letter from a runner whose leg cramps had yielded to vitamins C and E. At the time, I had given him high grades for self-hypnosis. But now, I was in them up to my hips. By noon, my urine was a bright saffron. The B-complex was at work. The last time I had taken that many vitamin tablets was when I was recuperating from hepatitis. I took so many that my urine actually became fluorescent, a reaction that startled even the doctors at the Rockefeller Institute who reviewed my case.

At night I would retire to a hot tub with some cracked ice in a plastic wrapper, and every so often would take the damaged limb out of the water and rub it with the ice. As I sat there, I would think of yet more remedies for this catastrophe.

Oddly, things seemed to be getting better. I was far from well and a long way from running, but I began to hope. And with hope came prayer. I began to dun heaven, to appeal to my lost saints. I prayed to everyone including the tooth fairy. I left nothing to chance.

Something was working—perhaps the Butazolidine, or maybe the C, more likely the hot tub and ice. It may have been just the passage of time. Whatever it was, my hamstring pull was beginning to clear up.

With the improvement came the resolutions—soon to be forgotten, of course. My reform would last only until I was running pain-free, and then I would forget to do all those things I promised. But for now I was resolved to stretch before and after running and each night before I went to bed. I would never allow my hamstrings to get that tight and short and inflexible again.

Two weeks later, I received a letter from a runner with a hamstring pull. He wanted to know about drugs and vitamins, about the whirlpool and ultrasound. Was there a chance, he asked, that massage and manipulation would work? By then, I was no longer a patient. I had become the doctor again. Reason and logic again held sway.

All that was just first aid, I told him. He must find out why it happened, discover what balance exists in his body structure and in his muscles. There is no real evidence, I pointed out, that any of these other treatments are of value.

Still, I said, you never can tell. Try whatever you want, and if it works let me know. Medicine, you see, is not only a science: It is an art. But that is something you have to be a patient to know.

In 1973, we celebrated the 500th anniversary of the birth of Nicholas Copernicus. We honored the man who first said the earth revolved around the sun, the man who wrote, "If we face facts with both eyes open, finally we will place the sun himself at the center of the universe."

That same year, a meeting was held in San Francisco proposing a theory no less revolutionary. The foot, said this convention, is the cause of most athletic injuries. The athlete, claimed this convocation, revolved around his or her foot. Treatment must begin there, or there would be no beginning at all.

In the early 70s, sports medicine was still a surgical specialty. The typical patient was one of Saturday's Heros. The typical injury was the damage resulting from a split-second collision of irresistable force and immovable object. The typical treatment was surgery.

"The sports medicine meetings I attend," a team physician told me at that time, "are really surgical conferences."

The emphasis on surgery to the detriment of orthopedic medicine had been deplored by the surgical leaders. In 1951, the president of the American Academy of Orthopedic Surgeons had issued this warning: "Because operations are spectacular, our residents often complete their training with distorted views as to the importance of surgery in orthopedics. They enter practice with but a vague view of the application of orthopedic principles."

This condition still has not changed. Recently, I talked to a young orthopedic surgeon with a professional team who told me he had learned more sports medicine from a baseball trainer than he had in all of residency or practice.

"Before that," he said, "I had taken the traditional approach: Make the diagnosis; select the appropriate operation."

But even then, the handwriting was on the wall. There were no longer any appropriate operations. We had gone from the sports medicine of trauma to the sports medicine of overuse. The typical patient became a common, garden-variety human being engaged in a running sport—jogging, tennis, handball, basketball or the like. The typical injury was the result of innumerable repetitions of the same action. The typical treatment was medical.

The problem now was too much conditioning rather than too little, overdeveloped muscles rather than underdeveloped ones. The basic cause was a structural weakness in the foot rather than an act of God in the momentary cataclysmic reaction between two opposing forces.

So orthodoxy failed. Standard practices were not enough. The athlete began to look elsewhere. "It is a well known fact," wrote South African physiotherapist C. Pilkington in 1970, "that a great number of sportsmen lack confidence in the medical profession and turn to quack treatment for a rapid cure." I felt the same way myself.

I began running fifteen years ago, before jogging became respectable. And it cost me days and weeks of injuries to learn that I, a physician, knew nothing, and my colleagues knew nothing. In my years of running, I have never been helped by anyone with M.D. after his name. I learned about feet from a podiatrist, muscles from a gymnastics coach, the short leg syndrome from a physical education teacher.

The roads became my teaching laboratory. I learned to use different shoes, different surfaces, arch supports and exercises. I discovered that running on the other side of the road could help, or running with my toes floating or even pigeon-toed. But I never put it all together, never saw that it all came down to maintaining a neutral position of the foot from stride to take-off.

That final illumination came from a most courageous human being, an ex-marine who ran in what he called "essentially agony" for two whole years with chondromalacia patella, or runner's knee. He had gone through the usual treatments—drugs, cortisone shots, casting—and had experienced no relief.

Such lack of successful treatment was the common experience of athletes who suffered from irritation of the undersurface of the kneecap. An editorial about that time in the *British Medical Journal* had said of chondromalacia patella: "The exact cause of this syndrome remains a mystery." And therefore the treatment remained problematical. The orthopedic surgeons who had taken control of sports medicine on the basis of treating one injury of the knee, the torn cartilage, were about to lose control due to failure to handle chondromalacia of the kneecap, the most frequent overuse injury.

The ex-marine was finally cured, but not by the surgeons. He developed some pain in his arch and consulted a podiatrist friend who made an orthotic, or support, for his foot. And that support not only cleared up the foot pain but, *mirabile dictu,* the knee as well.

Sports podiatry had been born.

The 1973 San Francisco convention on "The Role of the Foot in Sports Injuries of the Lower Extremity" met not to announce a new miracle drug or a new miracle operation. It met to announce the birth of sports podiatry.

The cry at San Francisco that year was body engineering, body mechanics, body physics. Butazolidine and cortisone were dead. The foot mold would replace the scalpel. Exercises would take the place of machines. Othopedic *medicine* would occupy the center of the sports medical world. The sports podiatrist and the physiotherapist would become the central figures in the athlete's care.

All these were set in motion when runner's knee was cured with a foot support. We learned then that an abnormal foot strike can cause trouble with the knee, and we realized that the way to treat a knee was simple: Ignore the knee and treat the foot.

If this is so, then drugs and shots and operations and even exercises aimed at the knee will predictably fail. And if a foot support can help the knee, what else can it help? We soon found out. An odd foot strike can cause trouble at three levels: (1) the foot itself, with stress fractures, metatarsalgia, plantar fasciitis and heel spur syndromes; (2) the leg, with stress fracture (this time of the tibia and fibula), shin splints, achilles tendonitis and posterior tibial tendonitis; (3) the knee, with tibiofibular arthralgia and, of course, runner's knee. All begin with a biomechanically weak foot.

So the sports podiatrist who could diagnose and treat these peculiar feet became the new leader. Orthopedic medicine, the non-surgical side of orthopedic care, was in the ascendancy. But the podiatrist and the physiotherapist would lead the way. They would fill the void that the surgeons had chosen to ignore.

As late as 1975 Dr. Paul Lipscomb, president of the American Orthopedic Association, saw this as a continuing danger. "What can we do," he asked his colleagues, "to prevent orthopedic surgeons from becoming technicians with little or no responsibility for preoperative diagnostic evaluations, or postoperative rehabilitation, and for the management of the 80 or 90 percent of patients who do not require surgical procedures?"

My own feeling is that the present way is the best. Orthopedic surgeons should be surgeons. Surgeons are born, not made. They have a particular personality: dominant, energetic, competitive, courageous, optimistic. It would be boring and out of character for them to occupy themselves with the routine medical care of the athlete.

We must allow every specialist to do what he does best, be it podiatry, physiotherapy, osteopathy, chiropractic or orthopedic surgery. There is a place for everyone on this team. The only requirement is that they be effective, and that the treatment be directed at the reason for the injury, not just the result. Nor should we waste time with treatments that have proven time and again to be ineffective.

We must accept, however unpalatable, however unexplainable, the therapy that is successful. "Truth," said William James, "is what works." And the truth is that sports podiatry works.

4

The Aids

Tried and true rules of the road for runners:

1. *Keep a record of your morning pulse.* Lie in bed for a few minutes after you awaken and then take your pulse. As your training progresses, it will gradually become slower and after three months or so it will plateau. From then on, should you have a rate ten or more beats higher than your morning norm, you have not recovered from your previous day's runs, races or other stresses. Take a day or more off until the pulse returns to normal.

2. *Weigh regularly.* Initially, you will not lose much weight, and getting on and off the scales will seem a bore. Subsequent losses should be in the area of one half to one pound a week. This equals 250 to 500 calories a day in output of energy over intake of

food. What you lose in fat you will put on in muscle. Running consumes one hundred calories a mile and there are 3,500 calories to a pound, so you can see weight loss will be slow unless you do heavy mileage.

3. *Do your exercises daily.* The more you run, the more muscle imbalance occurs. The calf, hamstring (back thigh) and low-back muscles become short, tight and inflexible. They have to be stretched. On the other hand, the shin, the quad (front thigh) and belly muscles become relatively weak. They must be strengthened. There are specific exercises geared to strengthening these muscles.

4. *Eat to run.* Eat a good, high-protein breakfast, then have a light lunch. Run at least two, preferably three hours after your last meal. Save the carbohydrates for the meal after the run to replenish muscle sugar.

5. *Drink plenty of fluids.* Take sugar-free drinks up to fifteen minutes before running. Then, take twelve to sixteen ounces of easily tolerated juices, half-strength "ades," tea with honey or sugar, defizzed Coke, etc., before setting out. In winter, that should be all you need. In summer, take an additional ten ounces of fluid every twenty minutes during the run.

6. *Run on an empty colon.* Running causes increased peristalsis, cramps and even diarrhea. Having a bowel movement before running and particularly before racing prevents these abdominal symptoms.

7. *Wear the right clothes.* In winter, this means a base of thermal underwear followed by several layers of cotton or wool shirts, at least one a turtleneck. Wear a ski mask and mittens. Use nylon if necessary to pro-

tect against wind and wet. In summer, the main enemy is radiant heat. Remember to wear white clothes and use some kind of head covering.

8. *Find your shoes and stick to them.* Heavy people do better in tennis shoes and basketball sneakers. High-arched feet do better with narrow heels. Morton's feet (short big toes, long second toes) may need arch supports in the shoes. If a shoe works, train in it, race in it and wear it to work.

9. *The fitness equation is thirty minutes at a comfortable pace four times a week.* Your body should be able to tell you that "comfortable" pace. If in doubt, use the "talk test." Run at a speed at which you could carry on a conversation with a companion.

10. *Run economically.* Do not bounce or overstride. You should lengthen your stride by pushing off, not by reaching out. Do not let your foot get ahead of your knee. This means your knee will be slightly bent at footstrike. Run from the hips down with the upper body straight up and used only for balance. Relax.

11. *Belly-breathe.* This is not easy, and must be practiced and consciously done just prior to a run or a race. Take air into your belly and exhale against a slight resistance, either through pursed lips or by a grunt or a groan. This uses the diaphragm correctly and prevents the "stitch."

12. *Wait for your second wind.* It takes about six to ten minutes and a one-degree rise in body temperature to shunt the blood to the working muscles. When that happens, you will experience a light, warm sweat and know what the "second wind" means. You must run quite slowly until this occurs. Then, you can dial

yourself to "comfortable," put yourself on automatic pilot and enjoy.

13. *Run against traffic.* Two heads are better than one in preventing an accident. Turn your back on a driver, and you are giving up control of your life. At night, wear some reflective material or carry a small flashlight.

14. *Give dogs their territory.* Cross to the other side of the road and pick up some object you can brandish at them. Never try to outrun a dog. Face the dog and keep talking until it appears safe to go on.

15. *Learn to read your body.* Be aware of signs of overtraining. If the second wind brings a cold, clammy sweat, head for home. Establish a DEW line that alerts you to impending trouble. Loss of zest, high morning pulse, lightheadedness on standing, scratchy throat, swollen glands, insomnia, palpitations are some of the frequent harbingers of trouble.

16. *Do not run with a cold.* A cold means you are overtrained. You have already run too much. Wait at least three days, preferably longer. Take a nap the hour you would usually spend running.

17. *Do not cheat on your sleep.* Add an extra hour when in heavy training. Also, arrange for at least one or two naps a week, and take a long one after your weekend run.

18. *When injured, find a substitute activity to maintain fitness.* Swim, cycle or walk for the same time and at the same frequency you would normally run.

19. *Most injuries result with a change in your training.* A change in shoes, an increase in mileage

(twenty-five miles per week is the dividing line; at fifty miles per week the injury rate is doubled), hill or speed work or a change in surface are all factors that can affect susceptibility to injury. Almost always there is some associated weakness of the foot, muscle strength/flexibility imbalance, or one leg shorter than the other. Use of heel lifts, arch supports, modification of shoes and corrective exercises may be necessary before you are able to return to pain-free running.

20. *Training is a practical application of Hans Selye's General Adaptation Syndrome.* Stress is applied, the organism reacts, a suitable time is given to re-establish equilibrium, then stress is applied again. Each of us can stand different loads and needs different amounts of time to adapt. You are an experiment-of-one. Establish your own schedule; do not follow anyone else's. Listen to your body, Train, don't strain.

Once our consciousnesses have been raised, our expectations are raised as well. Once I knew I could be a runner, I expected to be a good one. I expected to improve and to improve at a constant rate. I soon learned that such was not generally the case. Improvement is not automatic. When it comes, it is likely to be in cycles. There are soaring peaks, it is true, but there are also long and depressing valleys.

Almost every runner has suffered at one time or another from this Failure-to-Thrive Syndrome. It is an ailment that has three different clinical pictures.

1. There is the runner who just never improves; he is virtually stuck at day one.

2. Then, there is the runner who gets better but then hits a plateau; there is no further progress.

3. Finally, there is the runner who does well, builds up to a peak, sees excellence on the horizon and then takes a nose-dive; this runner gets worse and worse rather than better and better.

The most difficult to treat of these Failure-to-Thrive Syndromes is the first. It is also the most difficult to explain, and for the runner the most difficult to endure. No matter what he does, he seems unable to get up to any acceptable speed or mileage. While others are proclaiming gains in pace and distance, he is trapped at a performance level that is almost embarrassing. He is still trying to go four laps around the track without stopping when others who began at the same time are already talking about marathons.

A significant part of this difference is probably due to innate ability. Many people are taking on physical activity for the first time in their lives and have no idea of their inherent capability. In some instances, this may be limited. One way to find out is to use Dr. Kenneth Cooper's twelve-minute performance test.

This can be done quite conveniently by going to a high school track with a stopwatch, a whistle and a friend. First, warm up for ten minutes or so by walking and jogging. Then, have your friend start the watch as you begin to run the longest possible distance in the next twelve minutes. At that point, your friend will blow the whistle and stop the watch. The accompanying chart will tell you your relative ability.

Predicted Maximal Oxygen Consumption
on the Basis of Twelve-Minute Performance

Distance (miles)	Laps (¼ mile)	Max. Ox. Con. (ml/kg/min)
1.0	4	25
1.25	5	33
1.5	6	42.6
1.75	7	51.6
2.0	8	60.2

Levels of Fitness Based on Twelve-Minute
Performance and Maximal Oxygen Consumption

Distance (miles)	Max. Ox. Con.	Fitness level
Less than 1	Less than 25	Very poor
1–1.25	25–33	Poor
1.25–1.5	33–42	Fair
1.5–1.75	42–51	Good
1.75 or more	51 or more	Excellent

Runners who enter with a low maximal oxygen up-take are likely to make one of two contrasting errors in training. They either go too fast or too slow. Therefore, they have difficulty satisfying the three elements in the fitness equation. The running, it states, should be of a specific intensity, for a specific length of time, done a specific number of times a week. The aim is to do thirty minutes four times a week at a pace somewhere between easy and hard. This is necessary to achieve the training effect.

The difficulty is finding this correct pace. If the pace is too slow, it does you very little good. On the other hand, a fast pace is self-defeating. I have a friend who was in much this situation.

"I can't run more than a half-mile," she told me. "No matter what I do, I'm finished at that point."

A few days later, I went running with her, and we ran a mile and a half without the least difficulty for her.

"Oh!" she said, "I never run that slowly."

That was the answer, of course: slow enough to chat and still get that nice, warm sweat; slow enough to run for twenty minutes and then for thirty; yet fast enough to get better and better, fast enough to get that 25 percent improvement in maximal oxygen uptake that occurs with most running programs.

Runners must also be patient. They must not look for improvement too soon. Most studies show that the major increase in oxygen uptake and physical work capacity takes as long as twelve to sixteen weeks.

The essential, Ken Cooper says, is not to despair. Eventually, things will work out. Millie Cooper, his wife and the author of an aerobics book for women, says it took her a year before she could run a mile without stopping.

Like most runners, I always want to do better. I am constantly after myself for eating too much and training too little. I know if I weighed a few pounds less and trained a few hours more, my times would improve. But I find the rewards not quite worth the effort. My resolutions, so firmly made the night before, dissolve with the dawn of the following day.

I am forced, therefore, to do the best with what I've

got. I must get my speed and distance from the most efficient use of my body. This means, I have discovered, paying close attention to the three B's of running form: *big toe, buttocks* and *belly*.

I learned about the basic three by watching those who run the best and seeing how they differ from the rest of us. At a casual glance, most internationalists not only differ from us; they differ from each other. On closer inspection, however, you will find that from the hips down most world-class runners look quite alike. They can only be distinguished from each other by what they do with the upper body.

We can tell them apart by characteristics that have no particular effect on running itself. Think a minute and you will realize you tell one celebrated runner from another by the attitude of the head, the position of the shoulders, the carriage of the arms, what they do with their hands.

But it is what goes on from the chest down that makes for economy, efficiency and maximal performance. What they do from the chest down allows them to get the most out of what they've got. That is their secret.

We are beginning to learn what this secret is. The kinesiologists who study them think it has something to do with their increased use of the ankle. Dr. Richard Schuster, who has treated many of these athletes, has noted that their shoes are worn out under the big toe. My initial discovery, then, was my big toe. As soon as I emphasized the use of my big toe, I sensed an increase in power, a stronger pushoff, a longer stride.

I had learned the significance of a slightly longer stride some years back. I finished a twenty-mile race almost forty minutes behind the winner, only to be informed by an observant friend that the winner and I had taken the same number of strides per minute. What separated me from glory, he told me, was the ridiculously short distance I was airborne.

Not long after, I had another instructive experience about being airborne. I was watching the long jump of the IC4A Championships. The second-place jumper came down the runway, hit the takeoff board perfectly, but fell inches short of the leader. He had given it his best shot and failed—or so it appeared.

His coach came over and pointed out that he had reached for the board. His body had been slightly behind his foot. That almost infinitesimal check had cost him the necessary distance.

The jumper went back. He hit the board perfectly again, but this time there was no checking action. His body was over his foot. He won the event.

So there it is: You increase your stride by *pushing off*, not by reaching out. Never let your foot get ahead of your knee. Expend no energy in slowing yourself down. Save your major effort for your big toe. The big toe automatically brings the buttocks into the action. The harder I push off, the more likely I am to feel those big muscles around my hips come into play. The faster I run, the more evident is the post-training tightness in that area. A series of in-and-out 220s causes spasms in the buttocks that I never feel in a casual ten-miler.

What is happening is that I am becoming a sprinter.

I am using my anti-gravity muscles and increasing my ridiculously short airborne distance. I am also stabilizing the pelvis, keeping my back straight. It is the straight back that gives the thrusting leg the leverage for maximum stride. As the pelvis tilts forward, the runner becomes less and less efficient.

This, however, is only two thirds of the "B" axis. The belly also has a major contribution to make. When I belly-breathe, I add to the stabilization of the pelvis and the straightening of the back. I assume the running posture that marked Bill Bowerman's runners during his years of coaching at the University of Oregon.

As you read this, it may all seem disjointed. In practice, it is a composed, rhythmic movement. I begin with the thought that I will wear out the shoe under the big toe. This action automatically increases the range of motion at my ankle and then enlists the full power of the quadriceps (the group of muscles on the front of my thigh). The buttocks and belly now act as stabilizers. They keep the spine straight, the pelvis in the correct position.

I am still a little overweight, a trifle undertrained—but I'm moving like a champion, getting the most out of what I've got.

Every genius brings a message. Every champion teaches us something. When a person breaks a world's record, there is almost always a lesson to be learned—a new truth or a reaffirmation of an old one. What Sebastian Coe, the world record-holder in the mile, has done is to bring back relaxation.

Coe has all the other attributes of an outstanding miler. Like Peter Snell, he can run a fine quarter-mile and now holds the record at the 800 meters. He is light, less than 130 pounds, but has extremely powerful legs. With Coe, the footplant is not emphasized; it is the thrustoff that propels him that extra distance that separates him from the others.

But more than this lower-body power, the Coe characteristic is upper-body relaxation. Coming down the stretch in his record mile, his facial expression ranged from the casual interest of a passenger looking out of a train window to the serenity of a runner on a country lane at dusk. From time to time, he gazed over his shoulder—not in apprehension, but in curiosity about where everyone had gone. Then, his attention turned elsewhere. Never was there any indication that he felt the need to use his chest or arms or face to increase his speed.

Behind him, the best in the world were doing just that. They were beginning to tie up, the shoulders rising, the arms tight, the face assuming that "risus sardonicus," the smile in lockjaw, finally reaching that terminal state where they were using the neck muscles to assist the breathing.

I have a photograph of much the same scene in the Tokyo Olympics. This time it was Peter Snell, a smile on his face, driving completely airborne through the tape. Some fifteen yards behind him, spread across the track, was a phalanx of the world's best, each with a foot firmly planted flat and forever on the ground. It was the footplant that told as much as the tension in the face and arms and body. The runner's enemy, "rigor mortis," was setting in.

Coe was still doing what a runner must do to prevent this. He was running from the hips down. The upper body has two functions, balance and breathing. Motion of the upper body responds to and counterbalances the driving propulsive movements from the hips down. The arm carry has nothing to do with forward progress; it keeps the runner in balance. The arms, therefore, should be completely relaxed, moving just enough to compensate for what is going on below.

Breathing should be with the diaphragm. You fill the belly, then the chest. There should be no need to use the shoulders or neck muscles. Many runners do, of course. The result is not only wasted energy but also difficulty in breathing, development of chest and arm pain (the ubiquitous "stitch") and a general loss in performance.

After a race, a young runner came up to me complaining of difficulty in breathing during the race. He said he just couldn't get his breath and felt that he was overbreathing. He suspected he had "hyperventilation." He did. Hyperventilation is an excess amount of breathing in relation to oxygen needs. He was breathing more than was necessary for what he was doing. Usually, hyperventilation occurs at rest, but it can also happen while running and particularly while racing.

I gave him a suggestion: Pretend you are riding a horse, I told him. The lower body from the hips down is the horse. Just sit loose on that horse, using your upper body for balance. At the same time, concentrate on breathing with your belly and exhaling with a groan. The upper body, I pointed out, should simply respond to the hips and legs. It has no more to do with the running than the rider does.

When I was finished, he said, "I dig you, Doc. I'm a jockey." When I saw him the following week after the race, he told me he had noticed a definite improvement in his breathing and his performance.

The relaxation that we see in Coe—and that I recommended to this runner—is nothing new. Coaches have always promoted the idea of upper-body relaxation. When the educator-architect-designer Buckminster Fuller was at Harvard, he ran cross-country and was coached by Alfie Shrubb, a dedicated advocate of relaxation. "Stop running with your hands!" he would yell to Fuller. Then, Fuller would notice he was running with his fists tightly clenched.

I am aware, as you are, that to have someone say "Relax" often has the opposite effect. Try as we may, we find it most difficult to do this apparently simple thing. When this happens, it might be helpful to try doing the opposite. Instead of relaxing, tighten your hands and arms and shoulders and chest as much as you can for as long as you can. Soon, you will find you have achieved that relaxation you are searching for.

Paradoxical intention works in other disorders—insomnia (try to stay awake), for instance, and stuttering (try to stutter more). It may be an effective technique when your hands and shoulders and chest interfere with your running. You can, of course, always pretend you are riding a horse—or take another look at Sebastian Coe.

We probably would have grown to be adults with fewer food problems if our parents had not forced us into certain food habits which they thought were good but were later proven bad.

Young children are like animals; if not pressured, they will do what is right for their bodies. I once worked at a rheumatic heart clinic, and we were told to restrict the activities of the children. We never restricted those kids; they restricted themselves. They did what they could, until it became unpleasant; then they stopped.

The same would be true with food that is unpleasant to them. Milk is a case in point. People who do not like milk when they are kids never like milk. If they take it, something often goes wrong. I have ulcer patients who actually get worse by taking milk. People who come to see me with ulcers usually have been to other doctors. One reason they still may have problems is that the medication they take lasts only three or four hours, so by two o'clock in the morning their stomachs begin to secrete acids which again cause pain. First, they need a medicine that will last eight to ten hours. Second, they may have been put on milk, which they cannot tolerate.

I had one doctor call me recently because his son's ulcer was not getting better, despite their using the standard treatment—milk diet.

I asked, "Does he like milk?"

"Oh, no," the doctor replied. "He hates milk."

We took him off milk, and soon the son's ulcer symptoms disappeared.

Parents worry that their children will develop calcium deficiencies if they don't drink milk. Actually, it is very difficult to become calcium deficient, particularly if you follow a varied diet. Numerous cultures throughout the world do not drink milk, yet are not short on calcium. They obtain it from sources other than milk. In Cyprus, for instance, yogurt is a popular food. In India, it is ghee. Individuals who have problems digesting milk often have no such trouble with cheese, a milk product which contains the same basic nutrients.

One way to determine whether or not you have a food intolerance is to keep a food diary. Otherwise, it is very difficult after you have had some sort of reaction to remember exactly what you ate three weeks earlier when you had a similar reaction. If something unsettles you—diarrhea, nausea, headache or some symptom which makes you feel terrible for a while— you should suspect your diet as a contributing agent.

If it is something that happens intermittently, independent of your stress loads, milk or grain probably isn't to blame. It may be something you don't eat as often as those two staples. At the Mayo Clinic, they automatically remove from your diet shellfish, chocolate, strawberries and other suspicious foods. There are also skin and blood tests for detecting allergies. If you keep a food diary, you may be able to spot recurring symptoms each time you eat a certain food.

The way the food is prepared may also create a problem. For instance, raw eggs probably cause more trouble than hard-boiled eggs. Recently, I took an injection of flu vaccine, and it caused a tremendous localized reaction. Considering the composition of the vaccine (it is grown on eggs), this indicated I must be allergic to eggs, chickens or feathers. But I continue to eat eggs, except the morning of a race when the extra stress might be sufficient to cause reactions.

I have bacon and eggs almost every morning for breakfast. I don't know if everybody should do that, but it works fine for me because I don't have cholesterol problems. Maybe if my father had died of a coronary at age forty-two and no other male member of my family had lived past fifty, I would eat something else. That diet doesn't bother my system, and it sets me up for the day.

You get all your amino acids in two eggs. Perhaps I'm getting too much salt with the bacon and should take steak like the Australians do, but if you have bacon and eggs in the morning you won't have any blood sugar problems the rest of the day. (Hypoglycemia, low blood sugar, affects huge numbers of people.) By praising bacon and eggs, I am sure to get a lot of letters telling me what poor advice I am dispensing. But if you go back to 1900, people were eating this way and had nowhere near as many coronary problems as we have today. Poor health is more often related to lack of exercise than to diet.

You have to be very open-minded about diet, because people all over the world have so many different ideas about it. You should tailor diet to suit yourself. If you are the type of person who has high blood pressure and eats bacon and eggs for breakfast,

I would say you're crazy. You probably cannot handle salt too well and should be on a salt-free diet. If you have a family history of heart disease, you probably should avoid these foods. But if you have a family and personal medical history similar to mine, I see no point in observing those restrictions. Why shouldn't I enjoy myself in areas that are relatively harmless to me?

Bertrand Russell once said about philosophy that it occupied a no-man's-land between science and religion. I like to think that diet occupies a similar no-man's-land.

Dr. Henry Cabot, who was one of the great men of American medicine, claimed that when the final judgment is sounded and we know all the answers, the thing that the medical professions will be most embarrassed about is the diets prescribed for our patients.

And on that day of judgment, the cultists—the vegetarians, macrobiotic people and the like—will be similarly embarrassed because of the diets they've subjected themselves to in the belief that good health requires it. They sacrifice much time and money on their diets. If they do it because they enjoy it, that's fine. But if their motive is a desire for longevity, they are like the people who run solely to prevent a heart attack—only to be struck down on the street by a truck. They wasted all that time when they could have been playing a cello, seeing a movie or sailing a boat.

Almost no one doubts that alcohol has redeeming social value. It is by far the best means for breaking the ice at any social gathering. But does it have redeeming physiological value? Does alcohol impair or improve immediate performance? Does it have an effect the day after? And what are the limits of daily intake that will not cause any permanent damage to the body?

First, we must understand that alcohol is not only a drug but also a food. It provides seven calories per gram, calories that need no digestion because alcohol goes right through the wall of the stomach and small intestine. So at blood levels below 200 milligrams, a level that impairs heart action, alcohol is fine. Two beers an hour can provide a stimulus and a potent source of ready calories.

• *Item:* Runner reaches Boston College, the twenty-mile mark of the hottest Boston Marathon ever run. Says later he was near collapse. Is given, why no one knows, some vodka and water. Finishes in style, passing some seventy runners on the last six miles.

• *Item:* Runner in New York Marathon, his second in eight days, nears sixteen-mile mark in noticeable difficulty. Given twelve-ounce can of beer. Rejuvenated, he virtually sprints the last few miles.

What do such anecdotes prove? Nothing, scientifically. But they do suggest alcohol may not be all bad and that its use in athletics could stand more investigation.

But even conceding that alcohol in judicious quantities can provide both energy and fluid, what about the morning after? How about running with a hangover? What happens after a night on the town with little sleep and a couple of quarts of beer? Anecdotes here are as frequent as those about taking spirits or brew immediately before or during a race.

I recall a teammate in college who was carried home after a night-long beer blast and rose the next day to win a two-mile championship.

I have heard much the same story of a well-known runner who was poured into bed the early morning of a national championship and later that day won going away.

These were, of course, athletes who might have been able to win in any condition. But I have spoken with an exercise physiologist who tells me that runners have actually tested out better on his treadmill the day after a night of beer drinking. It is enough to boggle my middle-class mind.

And what of the longterm effects of six to nine beers a day? You're not going to believe this, but the literature suggests there may not be any. If your intake of alcoholic calories is below 15 to 20 percent of your total caloric needs, you are presumably safe.

If you run ten miles a day, this would add 1,000 calories to your basic requirement, or a total of about 4,000 calories. At 115 alcohol calories to a twelve-ounce can of beer, this would allow you to go up to at least six cans of beer. Prudence, however, suggests that four cans might be a better number. That corresponds to a pint of wine. Oddly enough, eight cans of beer are the equivalent of the liter of wine the French say should be the limit.

Having arrived at these conclusions, I decided in the interest of science to try them out. One Saturday night, I drank six beers, than ran a good six-mile race the next day. After a day off, I again drank six beers the following night. The next day, I thought about running but went home and took a three-hour nap instead.

5

The Trials

"There is no self-mastery without discipline," wrote Simone Weil. "And there is no greater source of discipline than the effort demanded in overcoming obstacles." It is necessary, she went on to say, that we hamper ourselves with obstacles that lead us to where we are to go.

My self-mastery comes from the discipline and the effort demanded by my personally invented obstacles —interval quarter-mile runs. Running has helped me in other ways. The long training runs, for instance, make me grow. Long, slow distance is long, lovely distance. Those miles are miles of thought and creativity. My ten-milers are no chore. When I finish, I feel ten feet tall.

I am using my body with intensity when I run long. I am reaching levels of energy that previously seemed impossible. I also am running with an absorption in my thought processes that puts me into another reality. I am listening to a debate which has, as William Gibson says, been going on since the day of my birth.

Discipline is another thing entirely. It is not a matter of being a good animal, of being a child grown wise; not something sprung full grown out of instinct or intuition. Discipline is not talent or intelligence, not strength or beauty. Discipline is the cement that holds all of these things together. Discipline comes from following what William James called "the still small voice," and thereby doing the ideal action—the action against the line of the greatest resistance.

I can't think of any action against greater resistance than repeat quarters, nor any time when the still small voice is stiller and smaller in my ears. Just the thought of interval quarters—a measured hard run, then a brief jog, then repeat, again and again—makes me willing to be a quitter and a coward. I approach the high school stadium with dread. I try not to think about what is ahead of me. When I do, I use the philosophy of Alcoholics Anonymous. I am going to handle them one at a time and not think about the next one.

I give myself the first one, hold my speed in check, look for seventy-five seconds on the clock. I stride through it, holding form through the finish. It's the last one that will be easy.

Two minutes later, I am at it again. The initial turn is faster. I feel good through the backstretch, but I have difficulty holding form at the end. Still, a relatively easy seventy-three seconds.

I jog around for two minutes. Then, back to the line and into the sprint. This time, I feel it at 220 yards. I have to go back to basics. Relax. Run from the hips. Breathe with the belly. I reach back for strength I never tap except in a race. The last few yards are in slow motion. Another seventy-three.

This time, recovery is much slower. I lean on the fence, catching my breath. I stretch a little. Oddly, stretching is getting easier. The speed seems to lengthen me out. Despite my resolve, I think ahead. I'm getting near the limit. From now on, they are going to hurt real bad.

The fourth does. Only the first hundred yards come easy. From there, I am holding on until the finish. I try to maintain my pace and keep my form from falling apart. The homestretch seems a mile long. Then, I am over the line. The watch reads seventy-three once more.

I struggle with the breathing. I am gasping fifty times a minute, and it's not enough. My groans fill the stadium. The legs refuse to move. Four of these are enough. But I am hearing the still small voice asking the Jamesian question, "Will you or won't you have it so?" The two minutes are up. The debate is over. I start my fifth interval quarter.

Again, I am a hundred yards out when I begin receiving distress signals. They come from all over my body—arms, legs, chest. Every organ, every cell is reporting overload. Doing seventy-three seconds is going to be a world-class achievement. I am breathing so rapidly that the air seems to get no further than my larynx and then come out again. I am out of the last turn and headed for the finish. But I can no longer coordinate my legs. I begin to stagger. There is no way I can last until the finish. I focus down to one step at a time, counting when my right foot hits the ground. Where it hurts, I make it hurt more. I try to concentrate the pain into one circumscribed unbearable ache and so leave the rest of my body alone.

Now, with the finish still yards away, I am reliving the agonies of other runners before me. No better description has been written than by W. R. Loader telling of his quarter-mile leg in a relay race against Cambridge.

"Dear God," he writes, "the weight of the legs, the revulsion of the tortured body for this punishment. These were no longer limbs that were being moved. They were inanimate projections, hard and massy as metal."

Still, as Loader recalls, there was no thought of stopping. "Remote in its eyrie, the mind cared nothing for the plaints of the body. Keep moving. Let's have no nonsense like throwing back the head and thrashing about. It never helps."

So it is with me—the same revulsion, the same will standing in judgment and insisting I go on, the same graceless finish, my face now contorted in that terrible grin seen only in lockjaw and at the end of races, my shoulders joining in the breathing just as in terminal pneumonia.

The pain is more than I can stand, and then I am over the line. I throw myself on the grass. My chest is heaving, trying to pay back the monumental oxygen debt I have incurred. I lie on my back and find the breathing gets worse. I settle for the knee-chest position, my face on the grass, my butt high in the air. Enough, I say to myself. No more. There is no way I will finish another one. I'll collapse. No more. Don't make me do it.

I finally get a look at the watch. Again, it is seventy-three seconds. I reset it and try to get up. Eventually, I get to my feet. There are thirty seconds before "go." I think of every reason why another 440 is unnecessary and irrational and even harmful. But my thirty seconds are up. I've reached the line. I start the watch and get into stride.

The first hundred yards feel easy. I'm trying not to think of what lies ahead. . . .

We had a five-mile race in our town. It was a hot, muggy day with a bright sun, little cloud cover and virtually no wind—a day to make use of every trick I knew about handling heat.

Many runners, I am sure, did not even think of the day as hot. For them, the temperature of sixty-nine degrees was seasonable for a day in mid-June. However, it was the humidity that was important. At 79 percent, it was high enough to elevate almost any temperature to a dangerous level.

When the potential for heat stress is that great, almost any race is a long race. Two years earlier, we had three runners hospitalized with temperatures over 106 after a five-mile race. All three had been training and were apparently acclimatized to heat.

The key to heat stress is how much fluid your body loses in sweat in a given period of time. The body adapts to heat by sweating and the cooling effect of its evaporation from the skin. The amount of sweat can be almost unbelievable.

A friend of mine who dropped out of a very hot Boston Marathon at the fourteen-mile mark discovered that he had lost twelve pounds, or five quarts of sweat. He was fortunate not to have suffered an acute heat syndrome. Loss of 5 percent water weight can lead occasionally to catastrophe.

The object, then, is to minimize this loss—to take plenty of fluids before the race, as well as during it. The most important ingredient is water. Only secondarily should we worry about what is in it.

For an hour or so before our five-mile race, I drank fluids, water at times, but mostly iced tea in quantities that eventually made me urinate. Only that way could I be assured I was in my normal hydrated state.

By now it was about fifteen minutes to go, and they began giving us the instructions for the race. There was to be, they said, one water station. It would be at the three-mile mark.

They were wrong. There were to be two water stations. One was on the starting line. Right there, I took six ounces of water and six ounces of iced tea. I was now ready for the first three miles—more ready, I suspected, than anyone else standing there awaiting the gun.

The race was the hot one the temperature and humidity promised. Fortunately, we ran on tree-lined streets and were in the shade almost the entire way, so radiant heat was not a factor.

At the halfway mark, I was struggling to stay with a group that was ticking off six-minute miles. Nearing the water station, I could feel them drawing away from me. I was beginning to lose ground to them and to the clock. Then came the hose and the tables with the cups and people handing them out. Most of those ahead of me took a quick drink, hardly more than a gulp, and went on. Some never even looked as they passed by.

When I reached this relief station, I stopped and stood there drinking. I downed two six-ounce cups, doused another over my head and then set out in pursuit. They had gained over fifty yards on me. But if the rules of physiology held up, I would catch them before the finish.

Water not only saves, you see, it also insures maximum performance. Keeping your fluid level normal also keeps your blood volume normal. That is what allows you to run efficiently. Passing up the water not only sets you up for a heat stroke, it does something worse; it makes you run badly.

And that was the way it was. Coming into that last mile, I made up the fifty yards I had lost. I was back in the pack and knew now I was the strongest among them. It was just a matter of being tough on that hill, and then I sprinted home with no one near me. My time was just over thirty-one minutes for the five miles, which was comparable to my cold-weather times.

Two minutes later, a runner half my age crossed the line and collapsed. He was taken to the hospital, given two quarts of fluid by vein and subsequently a quart by mouth before his circulation came back into the normal range.

What had happened was that he had taken no fluid before the race. He had heard, he said, conflicting stories about taking water. So he had rinsed his mouth out and then run the race. Had he stopped at the water station? "Just for a mouthful." So he had run a five-mile race in heat and humidity with the protection of one ounce of water. The result was near-disaster.

It was also instructive that he had felt no thirst. And that at no time had he suspected he was in difficulty. Heat is really a silent killer. The victim is down for the count before any warning comes.

The deficit in water begins at the gun, and for that reason we must begin to make it up in advance. Playing catch-up is not a game that works in hot-weather running.

Still, as my race demonstrated, there is a way to make hot-weather running safe, efficient and even enjoyable.

Running has always been a sport where effort pays off. Training has time and again made up for limited talent. It is also a sport where intelligence counts, where physiology works, where science is helpful, and where understanding what is happening to your body can make the difference between talking about heat stroke and having one.

Once I am underway, I enjoy running in winter weather as much as any other time of the year. The cold doesn't bother me. Once I am warmed up, once my core temperature has risen that necessary one degree, once I have reached my second wind, I run as comfortably as I do in May or September. The drivers, who pass by wondering why I am torturing myself, are no more cozy, snug and warm in their cars than I am in my running gear.

Running in cold weather is not torture; it is fun, invigorating, life-giving fun. All I need to do it is a little will power and some common sense. The will power is that extra push that gets me out the kitchen door. The common sense I have acquired through numerous experiments is dressing for winter running. I have learned through experience the rules that govern the choice of clothes for a run on a cold winter's day.

The best way to keep heat in is to use several layers of light material. Such "layering" allows the air between each layer to act as insulation. I like to have cotton next to my skin, then wool if it is cold enough outside, and finally a nylon mesh T-shirt which is both water-repellent and wind-repellent. I use nylon shorts for the same reason.

So I begin with cotton longjohns, then follow with a cotton turtleneck shirt. This covers the arteries in my neck. For me, this protection for my neck is essential. No matter how warmly I dress, if my neck is exposed I feel cold.

The lesson I learned quickly was not to overdress. When I do, I sweat so much the clothes soak through, and I immediately lose heat and rapidly feel cold. It is amazing how little clothing is needed on a frigid day. The experts estimate that the amount of clothing needed to sit around in seventy-degree temperatures is sufficient for running at five degrees below zero.

One way to avoid wearing too many clothes is to use some temporary insulation which can be discarded after the run or race is underway. I frequently use newspapers under my T-shirt for this purpose. As soon as my body warms to its task, I get rid of them. Meanwhile, my overdressed colleagues are stuck with several extra items of outerwear.

Another method of temporary heat conservation is to use the plastic covers that come on clothes from the dry cleaners. I cut a hole for my head and arms, and wear it. This is especially effective in difficult wet-cold conditions, those days when it is about thirty-five degrees and sleeting with winds of fifteen to twenty miles an hour.

Covering the head and covering it well is essential. I am told we lose 40 percent of our heat through our head. I believe it. For me, running without a ski mask is next to impossible. The mask warms the air I breathe, and then my exhaled breath keeps my face warm. In fact, one of the most enjoyable things about winter running is being inside that mask. It is also the answer to that frequent question about freezing the lungs.

The experts tell us there is no such thing as freezing the lungs. All the air that is inhaled is filtered, warmed to body temperature and completely saturated with moisture long before it reaches the lungs. Still, the mask is what makes me believe what they say.

After the mask come the mittens, not gloves. Gloves

separate the fingers, allowing heat to escape. I like wool mittens, but when the thermometer starts to hit bottom I switch to down mittens with a nylon cover. On occasion, I have used heavy wool socks either alone or over mittens and found them to work well.

Oddly, with all this attention to other target areas, my feet have given me little trouble. Tennis anklets seem to be enough. However, I do use leather running shoes which may give me added protection.

That about does it for my clothing. There is, however, another staple item in my ditty bag which I find indispensible in cold weather: Vaseline. I apply it liberally to my face, cover my ears, then work on my hands and use what is left over on my legs. Even where body areas will be under layers of clothing, I use Vaseline and have the impression it helps a great deal.

There is one other thing I must remember to do before I open the kitchen door: I have to remove my wristwatch. It has a metal band and can become so cold it is painful to wear. On a long run, I usually end up taking it off and holding it.

Now, I am ready for the road. I have enough layers of clothing artfully arranged to handle the weather outside. I have taken into account the temperature, the wind-chill factor, the presence of rain, snow or sleet.

What remains to be determined is which way to run. Shall I go north or south, east or west? At other times of the year, direction is chosen by whim. Here, it is by *wind*. The rule in winter is to go out against the wind and come back with it.

In running, as in life, if you follow a few simple rules, half the battle is won.

When I first came to Red Bank, New Jersey, to practice medicine, it was a sleepy little town. The newspaper was a weekly. It came out on Thursday and was read word by word until the next issue. The stores closed at 5 P.M., except on Wednesdays in the summer when closing time was 1 P.M. There were no Sunday sales except for necessities. Travel was by train, and then only to New York and back.

This may sound like the turn of the century, but it was only thirty years ago. Late-night TV was not yet here. The twenty-four hour day in sales and services and manufacturing was still in the future. Air travel, particularly across the continent and trans-world, was for the few.

In those days, we lived according to our circadian rhythms (from the Latin *circa dies,* meaning "about a day"). We followed the time kept by our biological clocks. We worked, ate and slept on a schedule synchronized with preset oscillations in our physiological functions.

Now, technology has changed the world. Everywhere, including Red Bank, the pace has quickened. Our schedules vary; Our days have become dysrhythmic. We are asked for peak performance when our body functions are at an ebb. We baffle these marvelous internal mechanisms by continually altering our time and environment.

This can be done, as it has been by many, by slipping into a life style that makes the night the major period of wakefulness. Mainly, however, it occurs through necessity in two ways—jet travel and shift work.

Each of these messes up our body clocks—the one by crossing time zones in a plane, the other by crossing time zones in our own home town. In other words, the shift worker can get permanent jet lag and never leave home. It is simply a matter of sleeping days and working nights, having to be active when every cell in the body wants to rest.

Jet lag has become almost as common as a hangover. Every day thousands upon thousands of professional people working for government or industry shuttle back and forth across the country displacing their twenty-four hour cyclical functions. The result is impaired judgment, slowness in recall and difficulty in making decisions. And when the problem affects a professional quarterback, the disastrous results may be viewed by millions of Americans.

In the case of jet lag, fortunately, the problem is relatively transient. No matter what happens, you are home soon and back on your own time. Pilots have learned to minimize this change in body rhythms by staying on their home time, and maintaining the same schedules of eating, sleeping and exercising.

In shift work, this cannot be the solution. The biological clock must be made to tell a new time and the body made to follow a new schedule. This is not easy, and shift workers are easy prey to fatigue, gastric upsets, duodenal ulcers and sleep difficulties. Researchers in the field tell us that the shift worker is less contented than the day worker. The most prevalent attitude is one of resignation and acceptance rather than adaptation and enthusiasm.

I have had fairly extensive correspondence with runners in shift work, particularly the graveyard shift. They complain most about frequent changes of shifts which make complete adaptation impossible.

One runner wrote to me about the effects of changing shifts every three weeks. "I feel like I'm commuting from New York to Honolulu," he said. "My mileage, which was 25 miles per week, is down to ten."

Other runners have reported much the same experience. "Rotating shifts is a disaster," wrote one. "Trying to change your cycles is a losing battle," said another. Even those with permanent night shifts have had to make some compromise in their training programs. They usually settle for lower mileage and less racing.

In resetting the biological clock and developing a new circadian rhythm, each shift worker does what seems best in getting the inner pacemaker to synchronize with the external time-setters. Some run right after work. Some take a nap, then run, then go to sleep again. Some wait until after a good sleep and then take their daily run. In this way, they divide into the "morning" runners and "night" runners we are familiar with in the usual day/night working world. No shift worker who has written to me, however, runs during his lunch hour. Running at 4 A.M. must be too dangerous or unpleasant even for the dedicated runner.

Two important elements in the adaptation to shift work are eating and sleeping. The sleep of shift workers is almost always poor. Special effort should be taken to minimize light and noise, and to reverse the usual social pattern.

Eating during shift work becomes a learning process. "The secret that I keep telling anyone who will listen," wrote one shift worker, "is eating only when you are hungry."

That is good advice for anyone. So is the suggestion that understanding the body clock is essential to all of us, whether or not we are on shift work or log high mileage in jet travel. We excel when we match our functions with our metabolisms.

While I was warming up for a race, the local runners kept warning me about what was ahead. I was in Denver, two time zones away and 5,200 feet straight up from my home course at Takanassee Lake. I had run this same 10,000 meters during our summer series at the lake in 38:40, a 6:15 average per mile. Now, I was being told that such a pace was out of the question.

"It took me five months to get back to my sea-level times," one man told me. Add a minute a mile, was the common advice. Only one person out of five in Denver was born there, so most of the people in the race had gone through this same adjustment. Now, they came over one by one to caution me. In this beautiful park filled with evergreens and bright sunlight, I was hearing nothing but bad news.

There is always a home-team advantage. Visitors have difficulty with the natives wherever they go. This is particularly true in Denver. On the ride to the park, we had passed the Mile High Stadium where the Broncos are almost unbeatable. The Denver Nuggets, who were sponsoring this "Go for the Gold" race, had a winning record at home which was remarkable even in a sport where the home-court advantage means so much.

Visiting teams had come to dread their trips to Denver and the routine defeats they seemed bound to suffer. They had tried many different tactics to beat the local champions, but none seemed to work. Some had used oxygen on the bench. Others had experimented by arriving at Denver at different times, just before the contest or several days in advance. Denver still prevailed.

My approach to the time-zone problem was the same I always use: Fool my body. Stay on New York time. Sleep and eat and work out according to my watch, not theirs. Then, get out and run before my body knows it has left home, the sooner the better.

I had learned from practicing medicine and running marathons that the body takes about thirty-six hours to react to adverse conditions. I have run marathons with distinction after being up all night in the emergency room. The sleep that counts is the night *before* the night before you run.

I had arranged the same sort of schedule for Denver: Arrive late Friday. Give the clinic Friday night. Race Saturday morning. Before my biological clock knew what was going on, it would be all over. So the time zones would not matter. It was the 5,200 feet that would make the difference. As the Denverite saw it, the altitude was the only problem. They hadn't even considered the time-zone dysfunction. The jet-lag effect was minor in relation to what altitude would do to me.

I had read as much as I could on just what altitude was going to do to me and how I could cope with it. Most physiologists agreed that adverse effects started around 4,000 feet. At the mile-high mark in Denver, I could expect anywhere from a 6 to 10 percent drop in maximum oxygen uptake, with an almost equal drop in performance.

A well-known British authority, L. G. C. E. Pugh, had done some very interesting research in this field on athletes at Mexico City. He had reported an immediate drop of 15 percent in their maximum oxygen test at that level (7,500 feet). One month later, the athletes still tested about 10 percent below their normal ability. Times ranged accordingly.

All I had to counter this ominous information was the same strategy I used for time-zone changes. Get in and get out. I had heard somewhere that if you are going to race at altitude, be sure you get there no earlier than twenty-four hours before the race. If you do, you will run better. Not well, just better. It was the only positive thought I had when the gun went off.

There were 800 in the race, and I stayed back in the pack, trying not to get caught up in the early rush. Even at altitude, the tendency is to run the first mile too fast. I aim for a pace I would be happy with if I were finishing. I ask myself, "Is this the pace I usually run toward the end of the race?" If the answer is affirmative, I stick to that speed no matter how many runners go rushing by. It is always best to run an even pace in a race. At altitude, it is absolutely essential.

In Denver, this tactic worked. I had figured the altitude should cost me about thirty seconds per mile. I could handle, I reckoned, a 6:45 average. At the mile mark, I was moving at a pace that my body approved. I felt really good, and then I heard the split: "6:35." I then settled down to holding that same speed for another 5.2 miles and having the confidence I could do it.

Then, I noticed for the first time how thin the air was. My legs felt fine and I was full of running, but the air was not adequate. It was as if I had ordered a milkshake and had been given skimmed milk instead.

Still, I kept it around that same pace all the way. At five miles, I was just ten seconds over the 6:30 average and even ready for a drive to the finish. What held me back was not pain, although there was enough of that. What stopped me was fear. I was willing to stand the pain, but I just did not know what would happen if I tried harder. I had seen world-class runners collapse at the finish of distance runs in Mexico City, and now I began to think of that possibility. Had they gotten any warnings? I didn't know.

So I kept it steady through that last mile. I came through the finish line hearing my time, 40:18. I had strung together successive 6:30s. I had astounded the natives. I had, as the gamblers say, beaten the spread, finishing less than two minutes behind my time at sea level. It was a personal triumph.

An hour later, I began to pay for the triumph. The

stomach cramps came first, then the nausea and then the fatigue. I was wiped out, unable to enjoy the hospitality of my Denver friends. All the Italian food and the Guinness and the good talk went to waste. I slept on the plane home, but it was three days before I felt myself again.

Denver, I decided, is a great place to live, but not to visit.

Part Two

The Play

Some Christmases ago, the school where my daughter taught kindergarten had open house. I visited her classroom. The entire room was covered with drawings of angels, but angels only a child could see and no theologian had ever imagined. They were of every shape and size, every color of the spectrum, uniformly joyous.

I thought, "Please, don't let them grow up."

An impossible plea, of course. We all grow up. We lose the wonder and imagination and trust that come with childhood, and then pass as childhood passes and are lost forever.

Or so I thought, until in France I went to see the Matisse chapel in Vence. Entering that chapel was like re-entering that kindergarten—only better. Here was the final, glorious manifestation of those childhood visions. Here was the work of, as Blake wrote, "a child grown wise." Here was all that joy, all that certainty and trust done by a master's hand. Matisse had transformed a room not much larger than my daughter's kindergarten into a world of flowers and light.

When Matisse wrote about the chapel, he said it was the fruit of a huge, sincere and difficult striving —not a labor he had chosen, but rather something for which he had *been* chosen. He had succeeded because he had learned the secret of aging. It is to become once more a child.

Later, when I visited the Matisse Musée, I was struck by this same progression in his work. The museum is on the outskirts of Nice, a villa in a small park. Immediately in front of it is a children's playground with brightly striped booths, a May Pole, and a small platform for games and dancing. I could sense already what I was to meet inside.

In the first rooms, I saw Matisse becoming that accomplished artist. There were the usual nudes, the still lifes and the landscapes done impeccably well. Then, gradually, I could see the bold line taking over, the reduction to essentials, childlike drawings done by a genius. The master expressed the uninhibited energy, passion and perception of the child. The complete control of his art allowed him to play, capturing everything in a single line and the simplest of colors.

This, surely, is what Picasso meant when he said it takes a long time to become young. The advantage of age is that you can become that child again, and better—for now you are a child who has the tools, a child who has been twice born, who has seen the worst in the world and yet who, like Matisse, is able to go beyond to the real world.

The young-old see the miracle that each day represents. True aging occurs not in retirement but in rebirth, in a new kindergarten, a new making of angels, a new chapel to a new and understanding God.

6

The Age

During a visit to Dublin, I had occasion to run with Noel Carroll, the former Villanova middle-distance star and ex-Olympian. Carroll, then thirty-seven, had never stopped running. At 175 pounds, he was almost twenty-five pounds lighter than when he ran for Jumbo Elliott at Villanova. He had the hungry look that is the mark of a champion. He was a completely functional unit of bone and muscle. For him, running was a fluid, incredibly easy motion. But underneath, you could see the power and strength he had available.

That day, he was doing in-and-out 200 meters. He carried us along, me and a half-dozen younger runners, mostly students at the University. He would jog down the backstretch, accelerate into the turn and then gradually draw away from us down the stretch.

After crossing the finish line, he would slow to a trot until we caught up. We would do twenty fast 200s in all, he said.

Five was enough for me. I stopped to watch as Carroll kept turning them out. Presently, I met a runner my age, and we headed for a meadow and a few easy miles. When we came back, they were still at it. The students were looking weary and were barely hanging on. Carroll was bathed in sweat, looking stronger than when he started. He was now giving glimpses of what he could do when pressed. He pushed the last repetition and left the other runners gasping far down the track. Then, he jogged up to me.

"Tomorrow," he said, "we'll do an hour over some beautiful Wicklow hills."

It was a remarkable demonstration by a remarkable athlete. But is Carroll really a one-in-a-million phenomenon? Does the fact that he ran a 1:52 half-mile at the age of thirty-seven make him an unlikely model for the rest of humanity? Or is he showing us the potential we have available but have never used?

I favor the latter. Noel Carroll is demonstrating what an international-class runner can do if he keeps training, keeps competing, keeps believing in himself and his body and what he can accomplish. Right now, putting the stopwatch aside, Noel Carroll is better than he was in his prime. But even in absolute terms, he is living proof of the extremely slow deterioration of physical performance with the passage of time.

Age-group world records compiled by *Track & Field News* lead to the same conclusion. From those statistics, we would expect Carroll still to retain about

95 percent of the ability he had in his prime—which is indeed what he is doing.

The facts, as *T&FN* presents them, are simple. When we plot speed against age, we find that speed improves up to twenty, is at a maximum between twenty and thirty, then gradually lessens beyond the age of thirty. Using world records as 100 percent, we see a slow fall in performance: down to 93 percent at age forty, 84 percent at age fifty and 74 percent at age sixty.

Still, you might say, these are world-class athletes, world-record-holders. What about the common folk? What relation does this have to us?

Amazingly enough, these statistics for world-class runners gave the same results as similar studies of large numbers of run-of-the-mill people in endurance races in Sweden and in the marathon at Boston. In both groups, there was a reduction of 7 percent in performance for every decade past their prime. Whether you are an Olympian or a housewife, you can keep very close to what you did in your twenties as the years go by.

I take myself as an example. At the age of twenty-two, I ran my best mile, 4:17 on an indoor track in New York. At the age of fifty, I ran a mile in 4:47. This was only 12 percent behind my time set nearly three decades before.

When I began running again in my forty-fifth year, I didn't have an inkling of what would happen. I was embarking on an expedition without a map or a destination. No directives were available for a middle-aged male searching for what his body could do.

At that time, there were only a few distance runners, and most of them were in New England or California. They were not ordinary men; they were giants—already legends in their time. I saw them then, and still do, as a breed apart, not common folk like myself. Most of them had never stopped running, yet here I was starting from scratch after twenty years off.

When I came back to running, I was the only runner in my town who was not a high school student. So, for companionship and competition and coaching, I joined a high school team.

What happens to a forty-five-year-old when he tries out for high school cross-country? In my case, I made the jayvee team. The varsity was too tough and the freshman a mite too easy. I had learned something: A forty-five-year-old in training could become the equal of a capable fifteen-year-old. I could push back the clock. The question became, how far?

It was a year before I dared think of running a marathon and another six months before I finished midway in the field of 200 at Boston. I had learned something else: A forty-five-year-old in training could run a respectable marathon. I could push back the clock, but the question still was, how far?

At sixty, I'm still working on that question. I have reason to think I am not that much worse than I was fifteen years ago. Depending on how much I am willing to hurt, I think I could make the jayvees again or, at worst, the freshman team. At the Boston Marathon, I finish about midway in the field. My time is only a minute or so slower than my first Boston ages ago.

Now, of course, I am no longer an experiment-of-one. These days, runners number in the millions. Collectively, we are finding what the aging body can do. We are gathering evidence on the natural history of the aging process. We are showing what is inexorable and what is not, what can be delayed and what happens regardless of the work we put in.

Prior to the fitness boom, all studies on aging had been made on sedentary people, those the medical profession used as "normals." Then, Dr. Herbert DeVries, a University of Southern California physiologist, noted that reports on the effects of aging made no allowance for fitness. It seemed to him that we had been given a false picture of the inevitable loss of function with advancing years. He decided to see what training could do for elderly people.

Dr. DeVries went to a retirement community and recruited sixty-two card-playing, TV-watching benchwarmers for a fitness program. He set up a one-hour-a-day, four-day-a-week schedule of stretching, calisthenics and walking/running in an attempt to make these people into athletes.

These subjects with a mean age of sixty-nine significantly improved and maintained cardio-pulmonary endurance. Testing after the exercise program showed improvement in work capacity up to 35 percent. DeVries proved that the sedentary sixty-nine-year-old can improve by the same percentage as the sedentary twenty-eight-year-old when enlisted in a suitable training routine.

This experimental evidence has been corroborated

by studies done at two major endurance events, the Vasa cross-country ski race in Sweden and the 1978 Boston Marathon. The fifty-four-mile Vasa hosted 7,625 male skiers with large numbers in every age-group, including the over-sixty category. The Boston run had 4,762 entrants and, again, had sufficient finishers in every age-group to make a credible statement about performance related to age.

L. E. Bottiger, who analyzed the Vasa results, came to these conclusions: The best mean time was turned in by the thirty- to thirty-five-year-olds. There was a decrease of 5 to 10 percent in performance for every additional ten years of age (actually, the fifty-five to sixty time was only 15 percent behind the leaders).

The Boston report was quite similar. However, in a foot race the younger age-groups always do better. In the marathon, the best mean time was set by the twenty- to twenty-five-year-olds at 2:51. With each five-year increment in years, the time got progressively slower. But the thirty-six to forty group still finished in 2:59, excellent time and remarkably close to runners fifteen to twenty years younger. My platoon, the fifty-six- to sixty-year-olds, had a mean time thirty minutes slower than the winning group. This figures out to only a 16 percent loss in thirty years—an amazing figure.

What can my aging body do? Almost anything if I want it badly enough. Given the dedication, the courage and the persistence, a sixty-year-old can become an athlete—and a good one. In fact, if you are twenty-eight and watching TV, you'd better not get up and look out the window. You'll see any number of elderly men and women who are training to beat you at your own game. Youth.

When I turned sixty, I reached what *The Amherst Student* in a congratulatory letter to Robert Frost called "that advanced age." Frost, of course, would have none of it. In a reply, he said he considered sixty no achievement at all. Advanced age, he stated, was somewhere around ninety, no less.

The World Health Organization, however, seems to agree with the editors of *The Amherst Student*. When I became sixty, according to the WHO, I was indeed elderly. For that institution, and I presume scientists around the world, sixty is a decisive year—a time to be excused from active duty, a time to retire, a time that marks the end of my effective participation in the activities of the herd.

No one—and certainly not I—wants to be elderly. You are, they tell me, only as old as you feel. Feel young and you stay young. I personally will have none of that message. How I feel depends on the time of the day and how long it has been since my last cup of coffee. Now, and for as long as I can remember, I awaken in the morning feeling like Methuselah. If feeling old means it is difficult to get out of bed, even more difficult to get to the bathroom and almost impossible to bend over the sink, I have felt that way since my youth. Only the smell of breakfast, the bacon and the coffee, has kept me from collapsing back under the covers.

I have learned to distrust feelings. When I feel my worst, I do my best. I have learned to push past the barrier of ennui and boredom, of lethargy and listlessness, learned that how I feel has little significance to what I can do.

The Pollyanna approach to old age does not satisfy me. Either I can hack it or I can't. Don't tell me about feelings, tell me about performance. Tell me what a sixty-year-old can do, what a seventy-year-old can offer, and tell me what's in store at eighty. Tell me about creativity. Tell me about my capacity to handle things like oxygen and boredom and stress. Don't tell me about being young; tell me about being old.

Despite being elderly, I am also an athlete, a distance runner. I know I am as old as what I do. What I need to know is, what is my physical scope? What is age going to do to me mentally? Only when those questions and other practical considerations are answered will I be able to accept all this poetry and mysticism about my coming of age at sixty.

What I need and want is a standard—something that can be clocked, recorded, seen, read, somehow quantified. Feeling is not enough. I want my time and place and how far I was behind the winner. Tell me what I can do and how well I can do it.

Now that I have reached the age of sixty, I have also reached a fundamental conclusion about my life: There's hardly anything I don't do better as I age.

That statement might not get too much argument from writers or artists, but those who keep sports record books are not going to believe it. An aging individual, to their mind, just cannot stand up to a younger person in an athletic event. The stopwatch is an unfailing instrument in establishing the difference between the young and the middle-aged, the elderly and the aged.

But what I am writing about is not a specific time or place in a race, although even there I am still doing well. There are days when I know I am a better runner than I have ever been in my life.

The truth is that every day I am born afresh. Every day, I recapitulate and add to and enlarge the person I was the night before. Age teaches me that. Each day, I learn more. Each day I run, I spend time listening to what my body is telling me. Each day, I am taught by the greatest of all teachers—the living, feeling, moving, tasting, hearing, seeing human body.

No wonder that in past cultures age was revered. Before technology, it was experience that was important. There were no shortcuts to the wisdom only the elders had, because experience could come no other way than by growing with the years.

Now, in the leisure conferred by technology, the aging athlete has become a new patriarch. Endurance runners with graying hair, wrinkled skin and birth certificates going back to World War I have become the darlings of the exercise physiologists. Scientists are endlessly testing middle-aged and elderly distance runners, and publishing their results.

What they have discovered, I already knew. My body can perform within 15 to 20 percent of its physiological prime. And I know from others I run with that I can expect only a gradual decline until I am in my seventies. Like most other runners my age, my body fat percentage is less than half that of the ordinary citizen. I also am able to take up, transport and deliver oxygen as well as any sedentary twenty-eight-year-old. My work capacity and physical performance is as much as 75 percent higher than untrained men my own age. All in all, I am operating at a level about twenty-five years younger than my chronological age.

Yet, for all of this, I am not special. I am a runner of sixty years who is simply getting the most—or nearly the most—out of his body. I am like all athletes of my age who are doing, not watching; growing, not aging.

Part of this ability to stand up to time is technique. When I run, I use biofeedback in its most sophisticated form: not with wires, gadgets and machines, but by letting my body teach me the most economical way to do what I am doing. This is the original biofeedback—listening to the body.

The conventional wisdom is against this approach. Either you are a natural athlete and do things perfectly without thinking or instructions, or you have to be taught from the ground up. I find both of those approaches wrong.

The natural athlete, as swimming coach Doc Counsilman discovered, usually doesn't know what he is doing. When Counsilman asked his world-class swimmers about their technique, they gave him answers which subsequent underwater photography proved all wrong.

The same thing happens with young baseball pitchers. When they first come up to the Major Leagues, they are *throwers*. They overpower the batters. Only later, with maturity, do they become pitchers. In the beginning, it is all talent. With age, they add the wisdom of their minds to the wisdom of their bodies, and only then reach their full potential.

I run my own peculiar way, my body's way. I try to experience the running and let my body direct the motion—with awareness of what is happening but without too much interference from the brain. I let my body self-correct. I let go, so I can feel what it is like to do it right. This teaches me to let go when I am doing it wrong.

I listen to my body in other ways. I treat heat and humidity, hills and headwinds with respect. I consult with my body when the elements become a factor. I have learned, for instance, that the best way to run hills is the way my body wants to run them.

I see age as an asset. Not a day passes when I don't learn more about my craft. Perhaps I don't learn enough to compensate entirely for the loss of strength and endurance that occurs inexorably each year—but enough so that everything except the stopwatch tells me I am now running better than I ever have.

There are even times, regardless of what year it is, when I beat the watch. I've been running since I was forty-five, but I ran my best mile (aside from my schoolboy times) at the age of fifty, my best marathon at fifty-five.

More often, however, I have days like the one at the New York City Marathon just before I turned sixty. It was a perfect day for an aging runner—hot Indian-summer weather with no cloud cover. Instead of running my planned 7:00-a-mile pace, my body held me to 7:30 throughout. But that was enough to carry me past hundreds of younger, more talented runners who had started too fast.

The time of 3:17 was okay for a fifty-nine-year-old. But now I'm sixty and expect to do better.

When Emerson was sixty-one he wrote in his journal: "Within, I do not find wrinkles or a used heart, but unspent youth." I am now sixty-one and know exactly what he meant.

Yet I'm not sure what led Emerson to make that entry, just what it was that alerted him to his continuing potential for growth. For me it was the announcement of the qualifying times for the 1980 Boston Marathon. Specifically the stipulation that runners over forty must better 3:10 in order to enter. There were no further provisions for age. No exemptions for those over sixty. No indication that the committee realized the toll that years take on the body.

My initial reaction was outrage. I had not run under 3:10 in three years and did not expect to do it ever again. I was content to be, and indeed deserved to be, emeritus. I was entitled to privileges and prerogatives that went with that status. I had run in Boston since 1964 and should be allowed to run there as long as I pleased. Asking me to turn back the clock was ridiculous.

Other sixty-year-olds were taking the same position. One of my aging friends had written a long letter to Will Cloney, the head man, asking for leniency. Pleading that Cloney make an exception for the old timers. Otherwise some grand old men, he said, would be excluded.

This grand old man felt the same way. When I read the letter I thought, "Right on!" It was unseemly to treat us heroes that way. We had paid our dues. We had been there and back. Yet here they were asking us to re-enlist and do it again. At sixty I was through with combat. I wanted out. Just give me a standing ovation. Then a quiet corner where I could put my feet up, drink some beer and give advice. At sixty everything is or should be settled. No more tests. Behind, the best I could do; ahead, the enjoyment of having done it. Suppose I could even beat 3:10; why should I? What would that prove?

Eventually it was the thinking that did me in. I began to see that the Boston people were right. They were, in fact, doing me a favor. Offering a challenge, and given the proper response, an opportunity for rebirth rather than retirement. They were forcing me to face the crisis of the sixty-year-old, which is no less than a third adolescence.

The feelings I had were much like those I had experienced at twenty and again at forty-five. Of being capable of more, but being afraid to try. Of being capable of more, but shrinking from the necessary hard work and discipline. And above all dreading being told what I was capable of because then I had to go out and do it.

The third adolescence is as difficult as the other two. The young fear failure. The middle-aged have come to doubt success. The elderly know both are false and it is effort alone that counts. For the elderly adolescent the major problem is getting geared up to go out again. It doesn't seem worth it. The lesson, then, is never give up. So I knew it would not be just for this once but again and again. People may retire you, but life never does.

Emerson, of course, had no doubts. A year later we see him going full tilt into the future. "When I read a good book" he wrote in the journal, "I wish that life was 300 years long. The Chaldaic Oracles tempt me. But so does algebra and astronomy and chemistry and geology and botany."

So I yielded to the Boston group. I accepted their unfair standard. I knew then this goal was good for me. It would make me the best marathoner I could be. It would lead me through this crisis to a new flowering, a new growth.

My first try was the New York Marathon. I ran well, placed well, won the sixty-and-over. But my time was 3:14, still not good enough. Two weeks later I was in Washington for another attempt, this time the Marine Corps Marathon.

Looking back now it is remarkable how easy it was. The course was flat, the weather perfect. A little band music before the start. The *Festival* Overture of Shostakovich, then the "Battle Hymn of the Republic" followed by the National Anthem. I had to be restrained from jumping the gun.

There was no need. I breezed through the first mile in 6:30. Then found a young medical student named Victor who claimed to have a clock in his head. "I am going to run seven minutes a mile," he said, "until I come apart." He turned out to be a metronome. And his pacing was all I needed.

There were a few anxious moments at the twenty-three mile mark when I thought I might be hitting the wall. Then they passed and I was in control the rest of the way.

The last mile was against the wind and the final 600 yards uphill, but I never had any doubts of the outcome. I crossed the line 783rd in a field of more than 7,000. My average time for the mile: an unprecedented 6:54. After sixteen years of running and fifty or more marathons, I had run the Marine Corps Marathon in Washington, D.C. in the time of 3:01:10, an all-time personal best.

The next day I gave a lecture on running at a college in upstate New York. Shortly into the question and answer period someone asked me what I thought of the qualifying times for Boston.

I stood there gazing around at the audience of students and faculty and townspeople. Surveying this assemblage of adolescents, some twenty, some forty, some sixty. Looking out at all that unspent youth.

Then I drew myself up and stood as tall as a sixty-year-old can without appearing arrogant.

"Eminently fair," I said.

After Montaigne read Cicero's essays on old age, he wrote, "He gives one an appetite for growing old." I have developed the same appetite, but not from reading Cicero. It is distance running that makes me want to grow old.

This desire to be a year or two older is common

among competitive distance runners. Alone among our contemporaries, we await with anticipation what are supposed to be our declining years. For myself, I found my competition in the fifty-and-over division too much for me. I wanted to be sixty and king of the hill.

That's the way it has always been. I moved into another classification, and I go from losing to winning. A birthday can change my post-race duties from giving congratulations to accepting them. A date on the calendar can convert me from an also-ran to world class in a new age-group. Add a year to my age, and I go from pursuing to being pursued; from simply rounding out the field to becoming the one to beat.

It is all there in Masters track, the world of the forty-and-over, the fifty-and-over, the sixty-and-over, even the seventy-and-over. This program takes into account the inevitable reduction in ability that occurs with age. It recognizes that small but significant decline of 7 percent per decade that takes place in running performance. It allows us to grow old with dignity and even delight.

The essence of living is wanting more life; not staying where you are but wanting to move on into the future.

Now, I've found asylum among my elders in the sixty-and-over group.

7

The Fun

When I began running in the early 1960s, I made two discoveries.

First, I discovered my body. I found my body was a marvelous thing, and learned that the ordinary human body can move in ways that have excited painters and sculptors since time began. I didn't need to be told that I was a microcosm of the universe, and indeed its greatest marvel.

I also discovered play. The great discovery was that this wonderful body was made for play. The books on fitness ignore play. They tell us "how to," not "why." They remind me of Bobby Kennedy's remark about the Gross National Product. Those figures, he said, tell us everything about America except why it is wonderful to live here. The books on fitness tell us everything about fitness except why it is wonderful to live at the top of your powers. That reason is play.

Play is our first act. If we are lucky, it will be our last. "The child's toys and the old man's reasons," wrote Blake, "are the products of the two seasons." We begin in play, and in our wisdom return to it. Play is a taste of the paradise from which we came; a foretaste of the paradise we will enter.

I discovered that play is an attitude as well as an action. That action is, of course, essential. Play must be a total activity, a purifying discipline that uses the body with passion and intensity and absorption. Without a playful attitude, work is labor, sex is lust, religion is rules. But with play, work becomes craft, sex becomes love, religion becomes the freedom to be a child in the kingdom.

What, then, is play? Perhaps even more difficult than discovering play is defining it. George Dennison in his *The Lives of Children* states that play is the perfect learning environment and then describes it:

> Let it be an environment that is accepting and forgiving; and let there be real pressures, and let it make definite and clear-cut demands, and yet let the demands be flexible; and let there be no formal punishment or long-lasting ostracism; and let there be hope of friendship and hope of praise; and let there be abundant physical contact and physical exertion; and let the environment offer a sense of skills and a variety of behaviors that lead to greater pleasure . . . and greater security; and let the rewards be immediate and intrinsic to the activity itself.

But that setting doesn't define play. We know play instinctively. Play is a peak experience, the feeling of "that which was, is and ever shall be." When we play, really play, it is unmistakable. Then, we become children and see things as they do, in their essences. Then, the present alone is true and actual. The moment becomes all time, the place we are in becomes the whole world, and the person we are with is everyone in it.

I have known these moments. There are times, for instance, when I come home from running a race in Central Park, and I don't know who won or where I finished or what time I ran. My family wonders, then, why I went, why I spent the day coming and going and endured the cruel hour on those rolling hills. I have no logical answer. I simply know that for that hour I was whole and true and living at my peak as a human being. That hour was life intensified.

Others are discovering the same thing, so the current popularity of running and other sports is understandable. What we are seeing is a revolution of play. Play tells us we are our bodies. It teaches us that all revolution must begin there.

Play is the answer—the answer to the unsuccessful fitness program, the answer to the unsuccessful life. Once you've found your play, all else will be given to you.

Some fifteen years back when the field for a distance run was usually less than a hundred, I ran in a marathon in New York where five of the runners were fifth grade grammar school students. They were members of a team called the River Rats which had been formed at the Tarrytown Grammar School.

At about the halfway point, one of the River Rats, his teeth gleaming with braces, went by me and soon disappeared up ahead. Fortunately, I was able to outlast the other four.

I learned then what I was to read in the texts later: The ten-year-old is one of the best endurance animals in the world.

The heart/body ratio of a ten-year-old, according to a German physiologist, is equal to that of a professional cyclist or an Olympic runner.

A later report comes from a Canadian, Roy Shepherd, who reviewed 9,000 tests of maximal oxygen uptake reported in the medical literature and made an interesting discovery. The maximal oxygen uptake, the best-known test for endurance, peaked for U.S. males at the age of twelve, an age coinciding with graduation from grammar school.

We have no need to worry, therefore, about children this age running races and even marthons. There is no more danger for them than for any healthy athlete. Heat is their only enemy, as it is ours. Proper attention to protection from heat syndromes is essential, but otherwise there is no danger in children running.

There are, to be sure, always the doomsday people. Now that fears about the heart and circulation have been put aside, there has been a lot of talk about orthopedic problems. Growth will be stunted. Other difficulties are postulated.

I myself see nothing that isn't transient or wouldn't have happened had the youngster not run. Runners grow or don't grow the same as children have always done. In fact, the runners who tend to do poorly later are those who develop too much and lose the physical characteristics that made them good at ten or eleven.

And if running is good for a youngster physically it is even better psychologically. Running which produces improvement in endurance and stamina and strength does the same psychologically. It improves the self-image and self-esteem and gives the child the opportunity to do something of value and even something heroic.

These are of primary concern to the child. It is these concerns that make children such a trial. They are continually comparing the attention they are receiving with the attention paid to others. They are in a never-ending battle to be number one.

They are, you might say, no different from the rest of us. They need to feel good about themselves. They need to be successful.

For many children, running offers the best chance to do that. Running is the right food for a healthy narcissism, the narcissism that says, "notice me, love me, value me," and then earns that recognition by being and becoming. Otherwise we have the unhealthy narcissisms of the real world which we feed by having and getting, a solution that always breeds failure.

Running is a positive sum game in which everyone can be a winner. It is especially productive of experiences where children can feel good about themselves. It is essential, however, that the children enjoy it. Running must above all be play. It must be an end in itself. It must provide for the child that magic moment where the world falls away. It must provide those experiences which are truly wordless. As much as possible, training and practice should be fun and should vary so that opportunities are given for runs in groups or alone as the child desires. Pain and fatigue, which can also be part of transcending and uplifting experiences, should be reserved for the race.

Too often I have seen these simple rules violated. I have seen, for instance, large numbers of freshmen come out for cross-country and then never come back. Their goal-oriented coaches were too demanding. There was not enough fun and play so they looked for some other pursuit their sophomore year.

Running is a low-key sport with many advantages. It allows everyone to participate. In running no one need sit on the bench. Every child who wants to run can run. And children quickly discover that the next best thing to running and winning is running and losing.

In a few minutes after a race it would be difficult to know who placed ahead of whom. It would not be difficult, however, to tell just who in the crowd felt good about what they had done. Everyone with a scant few exceptions.

What then is the problem with children running these long races? Simply that they will be turned off this wonderful sport and so lose what could be a lifetime of health and growth and happiness. We have seen it happen in other sports. We know of the tennis parent, the ice-skater's parent, and the problems in Little League and Pop Warner. And perhaps the worst of these is swimming.

I recall one Boston Marathon when I ran the last mile or so with a thirty-five-year-old dentist who told me he had been a swimmer at Ohio State. I asked him why he wasn't swimming instead of running. "I've never been in a pool since I graduated," he said, and I know that that is not an unusual occurrence among swimmers.

I'm always afraid of that with young runners. Will some parent or coach push them until they lose all the love of running and grow to hate it? Or will they lose interest and stop before they learn how much it has to offer?

We are a breed that crossed continents on foot. We were born to be in motion and in motion for inconceivable lengths of time. And what we can do, our children can do also.

We are also of a breed that has an inevitable drive toward the heroic. Each of us wants to prove that he or she is of value. Each one of us wants to prove his or her self. Children want no less.

Those who would prevent them must know something I don't know.

From what I remember of our block on Brooklyn, it wasn't exactly a melting pot. There were no blacks and no Jews, but we did have Irish, Germans, Italians, Armenians and one or two Poles. And we did have divisions, but those divisions had nothing to do with ethnic or racial or religious differences. It was whether you were a talker, a doer or a thinker.

In those days, these differences were evident every day after school when the gang gathered for the afternoon game. One group stood out immediately. They were the talkers. They had little interest in the game except as a means of socializing. They could spend the entire afternoon discussing what to play and choosing up sides. Talking was their real game. Should the game actually get underway, they still found the most enjoyment in conversation. In fact, the talkers would be just as pleased if the games were never played. Being together and gossiping was all they really cared about.

While they passed the time on the brownstone steps, the doers would already be in action. They were the real athletes trying to get the game underway, but in the meantime horsing around, bumping each other and generally trying each other out. For these doers, the day would not be a success unless they hit something or somebody. Football was their game, but they hung in there the rest of the year getting pleasure from flinging the ball against the stoop or whaling a pitch three sewers in stickball.

That left the third group, the thinkers, waiting quietly but impatiently for the game. Talking and horseplay didn't appeal to them. The game was everything to this group, which found in it the ease and assurance so difficult for them to reach elsewhere. This was a chance to lose themselves in a new and different world where they were competent and brave and excelled in something where it was worth excelling.

Those were the groups on my block—not based on the accidents of birth, but on the traits that really divide men and yet unite them as they did the players on my block.

Some, perhaps most, of us have come no further than that block in Brooklyn. We had people who wanted to settle an argument by punching you in the nose. They still do. At their best, these doers can be heroes. They are courageous, resourceful, adventurous, energetic and loyal citizens. At their worst, they are bullies and bigots.

The easy-going style of the stoop-sitters has carried them through the years, healing wounds and making the irreconcilable reconcilable. At their best they are friends with everyone, comprising a group affectionately recognized as the "salt of the earth." At their worst, they have become corpulent and sodden with food and honor and money.

The thinkers, always searching and never certain, have shattered false idols and ridiculed false gods. They have made everyman look closely at his own beliefs. But at their worst, they themselves have believed nothing, and have lost their loyalty to country and man and even God.

It is much easier, I think, to be black or Irish or Catholic or Jewish than to be a man.

"Man," wrote Schiller, "is never more human than when he plays." Play is the path to self-knowledge, the way to self-acceptance. If you would know yourself and then accept that knowledge, you must first find your play, and learn how to play it.

We knew that once. When we were young, we had no difficulty playing. We had sports for all seasons. Whether we were good at them or not, they filled our hours with interest and absorption and delight. We knew then what Chesterton meant when he said, "If a thing is worth doing, it is worth doing badly."

Unfortunately, we forget all of this as we age. I came upon my forty-fifth year no different from millions of others. I had forgotten the child I was. I was trying to be someone I wasn't. I asked the authorities, the experts, those with infallability, just what I should do and how I ought to do it.

Fortunately, the knowledge of the true self is not far from our consciousness. It is just that we won't accept it. What I had to do was to go back to play, to the doing of something that came naturally. When I began running, all of this came back to me. I ran like the ectomorph and cerebrotonic I am—enjoying solitude, delighting in reflection, finding peace in privacy, feeling satisfaction in the detachment that has come to mark almost everything I do.

Running, therefore, defined the person I am. It filled in the picture of the real me. It made me understand that I was normal. That personality is not a matter of charm and agreeableness, but simply self-acceptance.

Running can do the same for almost anyone. It is a universal sport. Anyone can do it. Anyone can enjoy it. I know there are some who say running is a bore, some who must hit something or somebody when they play. I have heard, for instance, of a rugby player who said he would play tennis if every third or fourth game he could jump over the net and beat the crap out of the other guy. And a headmaster of a prep school once told me they had lacrosse in the spring for kids who like to hit each other.

But still the fact that we are aggressive or tolerant or withdrawn has a great deal more to do with *how* we play rather than the game itself. Running can be made to satisfy these competitive, explosive instincts. Training must be hard and exhausting, and competition frequent.

For those who are more social, running must have social values. Training must be done with others and at a comfortable pace. Racing should be an event and it should be marked by good fellowship. Run-for-fun meets or only incidentally competitive races are needed. Group running can be decisive in the success of such a program.

Find the kind of play that fits you. Remember the saying: You can never beat a man at his own game.

In my running beginnings, I thought of myself as a member of a running elite. I saw myself as one of those happy few who were born to run. I pictured myself as the perfect runner: loner, interested in ideas, content to cruise the roads, living inside my mind, thinking myself inadequate for aggressive and competitive activity, supposing that I had little need for companionship. Function follows structure. I was built for running and little else.

To some extent, this was true. Running is the place where we born runners can delight in our own ability, be surprised by our own competence and find joy in a momentary excellence. But running does more. It makes runners into whole persons who accept competition and confrontation, into fulfilled persons who enjoy being there with others.

My running made me grow. It taught me to accept the paradoxes of the human condition, experience my own truth and act out the inner man. We embody truth, said Yeats, but we cannot know it; we must live it. To do that, we must become the persons we really are.

Running is basic training for that process. It is the sport for all reasons. It is play, it is exercise, it is thought and meditation, it is competition, it is community and neighbor, it is the self and the other. Running is not pure physiology although it can be, not purely psychological although it is at times, not purely religious although in certain circumstances that is its essence.

Running, therefore, is the sport for everyone. No matter what element dominates our temperament, constitution or personality, running provides an outlet. It satisfies that demand, and at the same time allows us to define our weaknesses and make them strengths. It supplies those missing attributes that diminish us and keep us from functioning fully. It makes us whole.

In the beginning, and perhaps even continually for some, running is not a pleasure. The discomfort and boredom of running are the price for the physiological marvels that result from it. For those who live by law and order, by gratification deferred, who see a desired fitness at the end of the road, this can be accepted. Commitment, self-control and hard work are part of their nature. For them, running is one of those purifying disciplines that the Greeks thought made you the sort of an individual a god might be willing to inhabit.

Others who have never been athletic, whose play

has been in coming together with friends, can find in running a sacred hour that brings communion with others. For them, running succeeds because it is done in concert.

But for everyone, regardless of the original inducement or the primary motivation, running becomes a ready means of self-completion. This is a state which philosopher Paul Weiss described as "the ability to master other realities while remaining yourself." It occurs most readily, he said, in sports. Running is the perfect sport.

The Mennonites belong to a Protestant group known for its emphasis on plain ways of dressing, living and worshipping. When you think of Mennonites, play is the furthest thing from your mind. The Mennonites are hard-working, no-nonsense people. They neither drink nor smoke. They are exiles by tradition and still see themselves as outsiders. In this fight for survival, play would seem to have little place.

Yet there I was, the guest of honor at the dinner celebrating the sixtieth anniversary of the Mennonite Hospital in Bloomington, Illinois, telling close to a thousand of these prairie conservatives about the importance of play.

Later, one of the chaplains would come up to me and say, "As I looked at the banner behind you, I thought to myself that we have done everything well these past sixty years except play." Later, too, everyone would seem happy with what I had said.

But when I had risen to speak, I was not sure how my talk on *homo ludens*—man the player—would be received. I had not been invited to speak about play. I had been invited as a spokesman of the 1970s to speak about fitness. I had been invited, the letter said, because of my preeminence in the field of physical fitness; because I had become a leader in getting people to take care of their bodies. I represented, the letter went on, one of the most significant health trends of this decade. Individuals were developing a renewed and heightened responsibility for their health and their bodies, and achieving new levels of health through personal fitness programs.

I did not deny these good things were happening. It was just that I had nothing to do with it. I was there, in fact, as a *representative* of those people—not as a pioneer or a leader. I was just another also-ran making fitness a way of life, just one of millions who had discovered play and with it all the good things the letter of invitation had talked about.

Ten years earlier in the same room at the fiftieth anniversary dinner, the Mennonites had honored Dr. Charles Berry, the physician for the space program. He was a representative of the space age. He spoke for the man of that decade—the man of machines and technology, *homo faber*, man the maker. As the sixties closed, we put a man on the moon and with him the promise of victory over all our other problems. Technology was about to save man.

That promise was never kept. Technology did not fail—but it did not succeed, either. The machine was not enough. Man had to enter into his own salvation, a salvation that had to begin with his becoming as healthy and fit as possible.

There had been a real fitness movement in the sixties. The program had been devised by a former Air Force doctor, Kenneth Cooper, who had even qualified to fly jets. It was fitness by numbers, a product of an age of diagrams and equations. It was absolutely correct physiologically. But despite that, it had only a limited success.

Man, it appears, cannot be programmed like a space shot. *Homo faber* knew the value of exercise but would not do it. Cooper's program, after an initial surge, lost most of its converts. People were content to sit back and enjoy technology. They agreed to let these scientific marvels do their living for them.

The seventies changed all that. The seventies turned our attention from outer space to inner space. The outer-directed sixties became the inner-directed seventies. Our problems, we discovered, were not so much in the world around us as in the world inside us. But this trip to inner space proved to be infinitely more difficult and dangerous than the one to the moon. The Sea of Tranquility turned out to be considerably easier to reach than that innermost core of tranquility we all seek.

What saved us was play. To get into outer space, one must escape gravity. We get into inner orbit the same way—by getting free of gravity and seriousness, by returning to play. The fitness that comes from play becomes the external sign of the child within. When you see fit people, you see people who have again become children, who have once more discovered play.

The Mennonites paid close attention. They knew

about holistic medicine, the treatment of the whole person. Their hospital was affiliated with a health center staffed by an equal number of physicians, mental health professionals and pastoral counselors. It was a thriving clinic with constant cross-referrals. The Mennonites knew the body and the mind and the spirit were one.

It was a small step from there to suggest to them that the mind and the spirit enjoyed play as much as the body, and that play was a natural appetite of adults as well as children.

8

The Run

When it comes time for my hour run, my body can't wait. It will accept no excuses. It interrupts my thoughts, interferes with my thinking and will not let me be. Once that feeling arises, everything, however important, must be put aside. Like a dog going for its leash or scratching at the door, it badgers me until I give in.

My body wants out, and I don't blame it. During the working day, my troubles are psychosomatic. My body is reacting to my mind, and my mind is reacting to the innumerable aggravations and upsets and embarrassments which go with living with people and deadlines and goals and obligations. My body is the victim of the tension and guilt and anger that go with failing to meet the demands of others and, even worse, myself. Before the sun is at noon, my autonomic nervous system is in disarray, and my visceral brain is about to throw in the towel.

Anything from a late start in the morning to a yet-to-be-opened letter from a lawyer affects that poor body. What I forgot to do or don't want to do or did badly is constantly reflected in the reactions of my body. The knowing observer can see it all: the shifty eyes, the hang-dog expression, the meaningless smile, the body hunched, the head tucked in, the slouching walk.

I know it in other ways. My hands are clammy, my head aches, and my sciatic nerve sings with pain. I am beginning to hear from my intestines. The belches are here, and I sense the stomach filling with acid. Lower down, the colon is in spasm. No wonder my body wants out. It has had enough of manning the barricades.

So the moment I suggest a run, my body goes crazy. It starts jumping up and down (inside, of course) and making joyous sounds (inaudible, to be sure). It begrudges the time needed to get ready. I have, on occasion, been known to start undressing in the car on the way home. My mind and will are little more than onlookers of this dash to freedom.

Still, once out the door my body accepts the leash. It is willing to wait for the second wind. So I trot that first mile, deliberately making it very easy. I allow myself to savor the initial feeling of release, to experience that sensation of escape. And then I am on the river road, away from traffic, alone on that silent road. I slip the leash and let the body go.

The Play 150

The Swedes call it *fartlek,* which means running play. It is simply the body running for fun, running how it pleases, running at the speed the body wants —easy or hard, fast or slow, jogging or sprinting, dashing up one hill and coasting down another, racing from one telephone pole to the next and then barely moving through the grass, feeling it soft and springy beneath my feet.

The body is in command. The mind can do nothing but follow. My soma is healing my psyche. If you saw me now, you would call out, "Looking strong, Doc, looking strong." I feel that way, too—strong and competent and a little proud. For once this day, I am doing what I do best and doing it well.

William James had it right: "To make life worth living, we must descend to a more profound and primitive level. The good of seeing and smelling and tasting and daring and doing with one's body grows and grows."

I can feel that good growing. My body and I go for a long ten-miler every other day now. Listening to it has convinced me that anything every day is too much. There were days, you see, when I took my body out whether it wanted to go or not. It was like dragging a reluctant pooch by the neck. But my body loves those tens. Even a mile from home, when you would think it would slow down and just enjoy, I find my body accelerating.

When I say, "Hey! Slow down and think of tomorrow," what I hear back is, "That's your problem. Tomorrow is my day off."

When I returned to running, I had quite modest ambitions: a mile or so on the ten-laps-to-the-mile track I had marked out behind my house. But that mile became five, and then I began to venture out on the road. The five became ten, and then I discovered the races.

With my first entry blank, I entered a new world. Before me was a cornucopia of excitement and achievement extending from the mile to the marathon. What started as a minor aberration turned into a monomania.

Man, we know, is never content. The jogger who is able to run previously unthinkable distances at previously unthinkable speeds wants to do better and better. The person who thought three miles an incredible distance and ten-minute miles an incredible pace is no longer happy with either accomplishment. The entry blank changes all that. Once a newcomer enters a race, there is a new set of standards, a new set of values. Play becomes sport, which is play raised to the highest degree in its demands and its rewards. Sport is play taken seriously. It asks for the individual's best and will commend nothing less.

Racing was an education for me. I quickly learned the facts about two new variables: place and time. I discovered that place was not that important. It would vary with the number of people in the race. The bigger the field, the more people who would beat me and the more people I would beat. Place was secondary.

It was time that mattered. It was those minutes per mile that I carried home with pride or disappointment. It is minutes per mile that bothers almost every runner. That statistic leads to the Failure to Thrive Syndrome, the runner who hits a plateau and cannot seem to improve. The complaint now is, "I've gotten this good. Why can't I get any better?"

When I failed to improve, it was not that I was training too little. It was that I wasn't doing the right kind of training. I needed the long, slow distance to build up my endurance. But I also needed training of the anaerobic kind for speed and for stamina. This is energy produced in the absence of oxygen. It is the ability to go into oxygen debt and not develop too much lactic acid. The best way to teach my body that ability is to do interval 440s or 880s at the pace I set as my goal.

When I finally accepted that truth, I joined a high school track team and began to do speed work two days a week with the milers. Five years after I began running, I ran my best mile of 4:47, and 10 years after I began, I ran my best marathon of 3:01.

What I discovered, and you should know, is that improvement is not linear. It is cyclic. I also discovered that training is not like money. You cannot put it in the bank and save it. You have to go out continually and fight again and again for the desired improvement. If I am to run a five-minute mile again, it will mean a lot of "bottom" work and a lot of painful "sharpening" work as well.

I spoke of that with Roger Bannister, hoping he knew of an alternative. I asked him about racing a few more five- and 10-milers or doing stadium steps, or perhaps some real long runs.

"George," he said, "you are avoiding the truth. Interval work is the only answer."

The worst-tasting medicine always works best. But like all cures, it must be taken only as directed.

I have a love-hate relationship with hills. I hate running up hills, but I love the feeling of accomplishment I get when I reach the top. I hate the pain going up, but I love the relaxed sprint down. I'm always looking for a flat course so I can run my best time, yet I look for hills, too, because I want to meet the greatest challenge.

Hills come in all heights, lengths and grades. Their impact depends not only on their shape but also on their location along the course. No matter where they are, they tend to separate runners rapidly. A group tightly bunched going into a hill is likely to descend in single file a half-mile farther on.

There are some awesome hills at the beginning of races. The worst I have ever run on was in Wheeling, West Virginia. After the gun went off, we took a little quarter-mile tour of downtown Wheeling, and then came the hill. It was a mile-and-a-half long with a relatively steep grade. Halfway up, I had forgotten about the race. It was just me and the hill, just me and the space of ground between where my back foot pushed off and my forward foot landed.

A limited focus always helps. The mountain climber's rule is "Don't look down." The runner's rule is "Don't look up." One upward gaze and I am overcome by the immensity of the task. The attention must be all inward—to monitoring the pain, correcting the form and living in that little area. I cannot live in the future that is the top of a hill.

In a race on a flat course, I have to maintain contact with the runners around me. I cannot ignore anyone passing me. On a flat course, I am running all-out from the gun to the finish. It is as close as running can come to being *mano-a-mano*, an eyeball-to-eyeball confrontation. Hills make for a different race. All runners differ in their ability to take hills. So the hill becomes my competitor, not the other runners. I pay no attention to whom I'm passing or who is passing me.

When I train on hills I use a trick the weight lifters use. They find the weight they can lift just ten times. If they can only lift it nine times, it was too heavy. If they can lift it eleven times, it was too light. I find the pace that just gets me to the top without stopping. If I have to quit on the way up, it was too fast. If I am able to keep going past the crest, it was too slow.

One time when I was hill training using this method, I came to a hill and gauged it just right. I ran completely out of gas right at the top. Only it wasn't the top. There was another rise that I could not see from below. I refused to stop and continued up, gradually getting slower and slower. When I finally reached the top, only I knew I was running. A passing motorist might have suspected I was shadow boxing.

When the finish of a race is uphill, it seems as if the effort and any consequent pain is doubled or trebled. The worst of these uphill finishes for me is the Cesar Rodney half-marathon in Wilmington, Delaware. One year, I came to that final torment a yard or two behind a fierce rival of mine. He was, we both knew, in twenty-first place. This fact was to determine our finish. There were, we both also knew, only twenty prizes. So there was nothing at stake at that point except one of us beating the other. I charged by him, took a dearly-bought ten-yard advantage and beat him handily. He told me later that he saw no point in battling to death over twenty-first place, so he eased in.

At the post-race ceremony, the meet director announced that they had somehow come up with one more trophy, so I got an award for twenty-first place. God loves runners who refuse to quit on hills.

I was on the third and final lap of a twenty-mile race in Central Park when I said to my running companion, "Well, at least we only have to run that 110 Street hill once more." He answered, "Doc, that's what we're doing best."

It struck me that he was right. The length of the race had led us to adopt a nice, steady pace. When we came to a hill, we simply maintained the same effort and ignored the slowing of our speed. I noticed that I was taking the same number of strides, but I had decreased my stride length considerably.

Somewhere, I had read that climbing stairs was nine times the effort of walking on the flat. Running up a hill was much the same. To keep the effort constant, I had to take very short steps. I was doing the same as a cyclist who shifts gears on a hill, again using the same effort but sacrificing a significant amount of speed. What we had done was to shift into such a low gear, and the hill had been virtually eliminated.

Since this breakthrough, I have come to learn a lot more about hill running. One indication that I am still using too much effort is a discomfort in the thighs. This is due to lactic acid buildup and indicates, among other things, that I have passed the anaerobic threshold. When this happens, I am using muscle glycogen wastefully. There is a good chance I will come up short in a long race. At the least, I will be running tired and hurt with the lactic acid accumulating in the muscles.

One friend of mine uses this discomfort to gauge his pace uphill. He increases his speed until he gets this sensation and then holds it there. I prefer to back off from that point and try to hold the effort just below the anaerobic threshold. The main difficulty with settling for this constant painless effort was the hordes of runners that passed me. There are any number of runners who pour it on going uphill, increase their effort and even escalate their pace. The worst thing about hills for me had been this feeling of incompetence as these people charged by. I finally learned to ignore them, and things brightened considerably. I now let them run the hills any way they want. I attend to my own business, not theirs.

My own business is running downhill. I always knew how to do that. I learned it in high school: Get up on the balls of my feet, lean forward, let go. Downhill, I'm a demon. Runners who thought they had put me away going uphill are surprised to find me at their shoulder, then past them and still going. Downhill, I let gravity take over. My legs are flying. Yet all around me are the strong runners who passed me on the uphill, now using more energy checking themselves than I am in going by them.

I used these tactics through college and then put them away for more than two decades. When I came back, I learned about distance running from an old-timer who was a bear going uphill. When we came to a grade, he would accelerate. He always took the hills in high gear with me struggling in his wake. Then, we would take it easy on the downside, landing on our heels and gradually recuperating from our surge up to the crest.

This style fitted him perfectly. He had heavy, powerful legs. He was a good climber but had no speed. He could not let out going downhill. I was, of course, the exact opposite and still accepting his way as best. It took a lot of years and a lot of races before I saw the truth. I was built to go uphill slowly and then race down.

I have tried to become a better uphill runner. Even though attacking hills in a race is reserved for the final stages, attacking hills in practice must be routine. That is the only way I will get any better in races where hills are a factor. Hill training develops my quadriceps, and the state of my quads frequently determines the level of my performance. Further, hillwork is what physiologists call "resistance training," which provides strength and endurance that can be gained no other way.

There are even more important reasons for running hills in practice. I can come to a hill and see in it everything bad in me. The hill is every duty I have avoided, every chore I have left undone, every decision I have put off making. The hill is my chance to rectify that, to do penance, to straighten out my account, to make a fresh start. That's what a hill is for.

When I run that hill with that in mind and heart, I am for a short while a new person. Good things have, of course, happened to my maximum cardiopulmonary steady state, but even better things have happened to my psyche.

At such times, I reach down and get energy available under no other circumstance. My body keeps going because I will not allow it to stop. My hands are clawing the air. My head is tilted to the side. Pain is everywhere. My legs are leaden stumps. The foot once planted seems immovable. Yet inside I am running. I will not stop running.

Once, as I toiled up a hill on a training run in ninety-degree heat, I came upon one of my townsmen standing by the curb. "Masochism!" he called out. "It's nothing but masochism."

Whatever it is, it's what I do best.

A reader told me about a peculiar experience he had on a ten-mile run. "At the 8½-mile mark," he wrote, "it was like I'd just gotten a jolt of morphine, a warm rush all over. I felt like I could run all-out forever."

"What was it?" he asked. Does that feeling have a physiological basis? Of course it does. On that day, and during those miles, he had reached his physiological peak. He had enjoyed for that brief time his maximum steady state of heart and lung and muscle endurance. Stress sought and applied and responded to had created this transient perfection.

I, too, have had such days—days runners dream of, days when I can do no wrong, days when the challenge of time and distance evaporates before my strength and stamina, days when I feel I can run forever and at any pace I choose.

One such day came after an Atlantic City Marathon which I had finished still full of running. Two days later, I went to a high school cross-country meet and ran successively in the freshman, jayvee and varsity races. I could have run until night fell.

Another time a few weeks after a Boston Marathon, I had a similar occurrence while running interval halves—surely the most demanding of workouts. But this time, instead of continually deteriorating, my times improved. In the final half-mile, I broke through some sort of barrier and ran my best time of the day.

All athletes know such moments, those times when they are at the top of their game and everything falls into place. Every athlete sooner or later has these occasions of putting it all together, of knowing the sensation of suddenly and surely being integrated with the sport and the environment—all conflicts are resolved and all doubts cease.

Why this mysterious fusion, this knowing you are one with what you are doing, this being for one hour the complete athlete?

For me, it began with believing I was a runner. When I was younger, my sport changed with the seasons. In our youth, we are available to every experience. Life is still an experiment, so we keep ourselves fluid in everything—work, friends, sport, life style, belief. Eventually, we must choose. We must concentrate on becoming who we actually are. We must grow. We must mature. We must follow our instincts.

I chose running. From then on, it was simply a matter of accepting the demands of becoming a runner. "Life," wrote William James soon after he had given up the idea of suicide, "must be built in doing and suffering and creating." I could see the foundation of doing and suffering and even the creating in running.

In addition to this discipline, I had the feeling of being special. Not everyone can get out of bed and run twenty-six miles of a morning. Those who have that ability feel special. We need that feeling if we are to go it alone. We need the support of self-esteem, of feeling our own worth.

Running also became my secret—another necessity for anyone who seeks his own way in this world. The individual, said Jung, needs a secret to support him in his isolation. So running and its mysteries are my secret. No matter how many times I write about it, the whole truth will never be told.

Running, then, is my discipline, my specialty, my secret. The golden days of perfection on the road are the wholeness that results, or at least the part of my wholeness that is physical. But it is a physical wholeness that fills my mind and soul as well, a physical fitness that anticipates psychological fitness. In those moments, my philosophy becomes, "I run, therefore I am." And on that basis, I view all creation.

9

The Race

I had just finished the Battle of Monmouth five-mile race, and was standing near the finish line shouting encouragement to the long line of runners following me. Where the race ended, there was a large digital clock so the runners could see at a glance what their final time was. From where I stood, however, a few feet before the finish line, the clock was not visible to them. I was there to alert them to their times.

"Come on!" I yelled to one runner. "You can break thirty-five minutes!"

Then later, "Take it in, you're 39:30!"

And even later, to an aging and overweight and very tired athlete who then broke into a broad smile, "Way to go, you've got forty-five beat!"

If you are a runner, you know how important it is to break those seven- and eight- and nine-minutes-per-mile barriers. If you are a runner, you also know that for me and the 300 other runners this race was not play; it was sport. We tend to use the words interchangeably, but there are essential differences.

Running is play; racing is sport. Play is the preparation; sport is the performance. My training is play; my race is sport in its purest expression.

You can see two of the basic elements of sport in the finish line and the digital clock. Sport proceeds within certain limits of time and space. In sport, there is an ending and then a score. Winning and losing are secondary to this absolute need for a final outcome.

In most things in life, there is no score, no objective, tangible, clear-cut measure of success. Ambiguity and doubt cloud day-to-day living. It is not enough to be told how good one is at writing or doctoring or lecturing. There is something inside me that wants figures and statistics and facts. For that, nothing can beat the race. The race is the supreme reckoning: a mark down to tenths of seconds, an exact place among hundreds of entrants, a course verified for accuracy, records for comparison, age-group prizes. Who could ask for a better ending?

This finish also guarantees another start. There is always another race and another and another, each pure and complete in itself. Sport is the perpetual second chance. If I fail this week, I may succeed the next. If this digital clock does not give me the desired answer, perhaps the next one will.

Play is only the preliminary to this world of quantifiable excellence. Play has no closure, no urgency, no rules. Play is doing a leisurely ten miles on a country road. Play is suffering through a set of interval quarters, or sprinting to one telephone pole and jogging to the next. Play is five miles of conversation with a plunge in the surf at the end. Play is freewheeling, uninhibited, with no boundaries of time or space.

Sport is, of course, altogether different. When I race over a previous training route, I am now aware that every step matters. A grade unnoticed during a creative reverie now presents a critical test of my pace. A hill not seen as a challenge becomes a pass-fail situation. Long stretches of scenic delight on a boardwalk are now miles of barely tolerable pain.

It is in this encounter with time and space that the runner is forged. The race makes me that athlete. All my potential becomes actual. I leave nothing behind, nothing in reserve. There is only the now, the here and me in the unity of this effort. Like most common people, I become uncommon only in my sport.

The nervousness and self-defeating tension that accompany many precision sports are rarely felt in distance running. Where skill and stretegy and chance are prime factors in the outcome, a player is likely to choke. Running, however, is not that type of a sport. In running, effort alone is the measure of each competitor.

The danger in running is worrying too little rather than too much. I frequently come to the starting line with little thought of what lies ahead. The race is a festival. It is meeting old friends and making new ones. The exchange of gossip and entry blanks for coming races fills the available time from dressing until the race starts.

So I forget the warmup, I neglect the stretching, I fail to get psychologically prepared for the challenges only a few minutes away. Then, the gun goes off, and I am overwhelmed by the sudden demands on my body—the swift onset of discomfort, the immediate aloneness that comes with every race.

When I get on the line, I realize that the issue is 90 percent settled. My recent training, whether I am over or under or at my peak, the state of my health cannot be helped. These factors are out of my hands. They are behind me. I need no longer worry about them. I have to remember only two things: one, not to do anything stupid and two, not to quit.

My aim in those few minutes before the start must be to create physiological and psychological readiness. The physiological preparation is simple. Ten minutes is usually enough. It takes me just six minutes of easy jogging to get my second wind. I then break out into a light, warm sweat. That means I have raised my body temperature one degree, and most of the blood is going to the muscles and skin the way it must for all-out running. I then do a few spurts at close to full speed, a few minutes on stretching, a minute concentrating on form and belly-breathing, and I am physically ready for the gun.

The psychological preparation is just as simple and to the point. The essential is solitude, a brief period alone with myself. First, I go over the course mentally, deciding where the bad spots will be. Then, I concentrate on what is really at stake here. I am in this race to do my best on this course, on this day. It is at that moment just before the gun sounds that I make those resolutions men make before going into battle. I accept what is to come with full knowledge of what it may contain.

Once into the race, I try to do the best with what I have. There is an old baseball adage: "Don't beat yourself." I must be careful not to run the first mile too fast. The race must be run evenly. Too much speed in the beginning and I will pay dearly at the end. I listen to my body, not the watch. After that first mile, I know exactly what I can do. I push to the pain threshold and hold the throttle there.

There have been races where this pace has been so slow and painful I have felt like quitting. I have wondered if there would be a way to drop out without anyone noticing. When this happens, I say to myself, "George, it is not your fault. You are doing the best you can." When I can identify with effort instead of performance, there is no need to quit.

I recommend this attitude. Over the years, I remember winning and losing races, but mostly I remember giving the race my best shot. I will not deny that my few virtuoso performances have helped tide me over some barren stretches. But I know that some of my best races where those in which I ran poor times. It is an old story: We hate to suffer, but afterward we are glad we did.

One reviewer has written that Tim Gallwey's *The Inner Game of Tennis* is no less than a new approach to living. If used successfully, it could eliminate anxiety, self-consciousness and self-defeating apprehension. By applying your inner game of tennis to your life, you would redefine success, purpose and ambition, and you could satisfy desires that seem insatiable.

I'm sure that was Gallwey's purpose. His main interest, of course, is tennis. Tennis is his play, as mine is running. But he also sees tennis as a laboratory where he has learned much about himself and life. His book is as much an instruction on living as it is on tennis.

It all starts, however, with the outer game. For Gallwey, this outer game is "played against an external opponent to overcome external obstacles to reach an external goal." This obviously applies equally to running and other sports.

The outer game is talent, technique and training. It is the development and application of skills. Over the years, I have done that with my running. It is a skill my body has acquired.

I know how to run uphill, how to run dowhill, how to breathe, how to carry my arms. I have learned what to do with my hips and my thighs and calf muscles, what is right for my ankle and even my big toe. I have found that tightening any muscle above the hips is useless, and that the upper body is used only for breathing and balance.

The outer game is a matter of achieving the greatest speed and the greatest endurance with the least effort, running the best race at the least cost, reaching as close as possible to that point where there is nothing left, neither ignoring nor being deterred by pain.

But then the inner "me" intrudes. My mind enters the race. The real race takes place in the mind, and here the obstacles are more formidable. Here, the opponent is not the runner next to me but myself, not the pain now but the pain to come, not the pain felt but the pain feared. Here, I am my own enemy.

The inner game, then, is an encounter with the doubts and indecisions that prevent me from being myself, from reaching my potential. The inner game is a contest with my inclination to do less than my best.

We all have that inner voice that says, "I think I can't." It must be stilled. The first thing I must do is to accept the commitment of the race, to determine that I will finish no matter what. This alone is a tremendous help.

That is, however, only part of the answer. The full answer, says Gallwey, is relaxed concentration. I agree. To do my best, I must concentrate, focus down on each step, on every yard. Yet I must not interfere. This is the relaxation, the acceptance.

Such concentration and relaxation can be obtained in tennis by concentrating on the ball. Gallwey suggests that the player say "bounce" every time the ball hits the ground, then say "hit" each time it strikes either racket.

When my inner game falters and my outer game goes with it, when my concentration wanders, I use my own running version. I say "bounce" each time my left foot hits the ground and "hit" when I drive off with my right. This little practice brings me back to that five feet or so I travel with each racing stride. It erases the worry that if I feel this bad now, what will I feel like three miles from here? And it allows me to view with almost clinical detachment the fact that the water tower at the finish line seems no closer than it did ten minutes ago. I can focus down on each yard like a wide receiver who sees only the football while knowing full well that he will be clobbered after he makes the catch.

My mind will have none of this nonsense. My mind knows how much I hate to suffer, knows I have always taken the easy way out. My mind recites a litany of my faults, my limitations, my imperfections. It suggests that I slow down, take it easy.

But oddly, I never do. And neither do those around me. I have beaten many runners, but none because they quit. We have mastered the inner game of running, and we are all winners. For a sweet hour or two, it seems we have also mastered the inner game of life.

The desire to run comes from deep within us—from the unconscious, the intuitive, the instinctive. And that desire becomes a passion when the runner learns to race. Then, the race becomes all—the lovemaking of the runner. The feeling after a ten-miler truly run is something beyond his previous experience. But that heightened feeling is just an overture for the marathon.

Eventually, every runner begins to hear that tune, the marathon singing in his head. From then on, the marathon is background music. From the time I began to enjoy running, I heard that theme. From the time I could run five miles and think it nothing, the marathon was an urgent rhythm in my body. From the time I raced ten miles and knew the benediction that followed, I knew I would not rest until I met the challenge of the absolute distance. The music swelled and became insistent in my ears, a melody of craft and courage, of weakness and power, of being alone and vulnerable and naked and helpless, and yet finally of overcoming.

In time, I have come to know my craft and come to know my body. I now see time and space in a special way. I am concerned with seconds and minutes and hours as are few others. I am interested in bones and muscles and heart beats; in oxygen taken in and sweat passed out; in all the things the body does that can be measured and charted and analyzed. I have learned about lactic acid and muscle glycogen and how aerobic differs from anaerobic metabolism.

But most of all, I have studied how to run a marathon: how to train (ten miles Tuesday and Thursday, and a race on Sunday); what to do before the race (rest for three days and eat carbohydrates); what shoes to wear (training shoes; what you lose in weight you gain in support and shock absorption); what pace to start at (my easy training pace); when to accelerate (at five to seven miles, reach for your best pace); and the proper attitude (concentrate on each step; know every minute you are running a marathon).

I became ready for the part of the marathon that is pure body. But the marathon is much more. It is, to use Yeats' description of poetry, "blood, imagination and intellect brought together." The marathoner becomes the total person, the total runner running the total race.

When I run a marathon, I put myself at the center of my life, the center of my universe. I know my life is not my body or mind or heart. It is what I do and why I am doing it. For these hours, I move past ideas of food and sleep and shelter and sexual fulfillment and my other basic drives. I bring my life and its meaning down to this struggle, this supreme effort which I must do myself without help from anyone.

But because the marathon is allegory and myth and history, I am not alone. At the very time when I assert my own self and achieve a solitary state, I join my fellow runners, become part of the people who run with me, accept identification with others. And why? I'm not sure, but it probably has to do with the story of the people. What we do must not be ignored just because we are not great men. Each marathon is part of our present and becomes part of our past. It is embodied in the memory of those who ran, and those who saw or heard, whether they know our music or not.

The music of the marathon is a powerful martial strain, one of those tunes of glory. It asks us to forsake pleasures, to discipline the body, to find courage, to renew faith and to become one's own person, utterly and completely. And then it asks us to give up that prize and join the whole human race.

Near the twenty-three mile mark of the New York Marathon, the course turns off Fifth Avenue into Central Park. The runners face a short but fairly steep and demanding hill, and then the course follows the undulating road through the park toward the finish.

I entered the park in the grip of the inexpressible fatigue that comes at that stage in the race. I was once again engaged in the struggle between a completely exhausted body and a yet undefeated will. I ran toward that hill, realizing that finishing was still problematical, fearing that I might still have to walk, and knowing that no matter what happened those final twenty-five or more minutes would constitute my most painful experience this side of major surgery.

I ascended the hill past a small group of onlookers. One of them recognized me and called out, "Dr. Sheehan, what would Emerson have said now?"

I had to laugh, even in that pain. It was a particularly deft shot at someone who had used other people's words to express his own truth—and I was now in a situation that clearly no one else could describe. But the question also went to the question of why I run marathons.

The case for distance running cannot be stated simply, even by its adherents. No matter how often I'm asked, even in more favorably circumstances than the twenty-three-mile mark of a marathon, my answer is always inadequate.

I am not alone in this inadequacy. At that same marathon, a questionnaire was distributed asking the entrants why they ran. The series of suggested answers had been made up by scientists of the body and mind. There were fifteen possible choices, the last one being, "Don't really know." The range of answers indicated the researchers' own indecision, their inability to put their fingers on their personal motivations.

I think it instructive, however, that only three of the answers—"Improving physical health," "Improving sexual capacity" and "Acquiring a youthful appearance"—had to do with the body. All the others (except the final disclaimer of not knowing at all) were psychological benefits. Runners apparently take as a given truth that physical health is a by-product of running but not the real reason they run.

I am aware of that also. I am my body. What I do begins there. But I am much more besides. What happens to my body has an enormous effect on my heart and mind. When I run, I become of necessity a good animal, but I also become for less obvious and even mysterious reasons a good person. I become, in some uncanny way, complete. Perhaps it has something to do with a sense of success and mastery over this art of running.

The scientists tried to express this in their suggested answers. Do I run, they asked, to relax, to relieve boredom or to improve my mental health? Is it possible, they inquired, that I do it to achieve recognition or to master a challenge or to find an additional purpose in life? Perhaps running, the questionnaire went on, is something I do for friendship and association, or because I am unhappy and unfulfilled without it.

What we were being asked was the familiar "either/ or." Is it process or product that pushes us? Is it what happens while we run or what we achieve through running that motivates us? Is running for the body or the spirit?

My running is not either/or. It is all these reasons and more. Running is indeed product. It is done for the goal—the ability to run a marathon, the having done it. But it is the process as well. Training is not only a means; it is an end in itself. The achievement is not the whole reason. There is also what goes on before the attainment of that achievement, what goes on before the mastering of the challenge, what is gone through in finding an additional purpose in life.

My running is both process and product. Sometimes, it is all meaning and no purpose. Other times, it is all purpose and no meaning. Sometimes, it is work, other times play, and there are even times when it is an act of love.

We who run are different from those who merely study us. We are out there experiencing what they are trying to put into words. We know what they are merely trying to know. They are seeking belief, while we already believe. Our difficulty is in expressing the whole truth of that experience, that knowledge, that belief.

So I wish Emerson had run marathons, and somewhere around the twenty-three mile mark a friend had asked him, "What's it all about, Waldo?"

Part Three

The Work

When Herbert Howe was preparing for his doctorate at Harvard, he learned he had cancer. Radiation and chemotherapy were begun. That was his physician's reaction, the scientific one. Howe's reaction was the intuitive one. He became an athlete. With an 80 percent chance he would be dead in five years, he committed the greater part of each day to sports.

"I swam an hour a day," he reports, "furiously punched the heavy bag and ran consistent six-mile miles over a twelve-mile course."

Eventually, he took up skateboarding, hang-gliding and scuba diving. Shortly after the chemotherapy ended, he completed the world's longest one-day canoe race. When he finished the seventy-two miles, he collapsed and spent three hours in the emergency room.

Why all this? Why, faced with pain in the future, seek more pain now? Why, faced with death, take the chance of hastening it? Why push on and struggle when he could take the time to enjoy life?

Howe sees no incompatibility between pain and joy. For him, they coexist. "I had to believe that my body was not decaying," he writes. "I had to believe I was winning."

Then, he quotes Michael Novak on winning as "a form of thumbing your nose, for the moment, at the cancers and diseases that, in the end, strike us all down."

To keep from decaying, to be a winner, the athlete must accept pain—not only accept it but look for it, live with it, learn not to fear it.

Herbert Howe decided to do more and more, to work harder and harder no matter how much it hurt. He then found that perseverance and pride became synonymous. Significantly, he notes, "I gained new confidence." Confidence and, of course, faith and trust grew out of the new man. He had reached a point where his experiment and experience had earned him self-certainty, self-trust, self-reliance.

Howe plunged on. He had come to see his chemotherapy and his doctoral dissertation as two marathon events. Since, he says, pride lasts longer than pain, he pushed on harder than ever before. He was supported and sustained in this by the discipline and absorption of his athletics. He was made whole by the fact that he had gone out to meet pain and grasped it, and having defeated his self-doubts about his physical condition he was ready to face the uncertainty that lay ahead.

Herbert Howe had discovered the athlete's secret, a secret they all share and cannot really express. For one thing, pain is always personal. One's pain cannot be felt by another. No matter how earnest the desire to communicate it, the effort falls short. We can almost, but not quite, understand the total reaction of the protesting body, the undecided will, the questioning reason, the hopeful and courageous heart.

Because it is personal, private and secret, pain is a subject that has baffled theologians, frustrated philosophers, sent psychiatrists to other psychiatrists and caused thinkers to wonder how much the mind can explain. Somewhere inside of pain and suffering is the mystery of existence.

Most of us can see the biological necessity of pain. It protects us, keeps us out of harm's way. Pain is nature's early-warning system.

Very few of us, however, can imagine pain as a logical necessity. Josiah Royce, almost as much a theologian as a philosopher, wrote of pain that way. Through our suffering, he declared, God suffers. God must suffer to be whole and just, and so must we.

Royce's theory is unique, as far as I can see. It is much more common for people to see evil and pain as the expressions of a bad body, due to Original Sin. There are others who see pain simply as a bad joke.

For the athlete, pain is neither of these. His life is good, and to live it well is to suffer well. He recognizes his pain as necessary.

"Live in the uncomfortable zone," a man once advised me, "and when you die you will have no regrets."

For one thing, you will have lived, tried everything, discovered your limits. And there is always the chance that you will do what Herbert Howe did: combine pain with joy, and discover that you and your life have no limits.

10

The Effort

There is a general feeling that people who have reached sixty should take it easy; they have paid their dues and are entitled to relax. Nothing could be further from the truth. There is never a time to take it easy, never a time we can relax.

Whether you are eighteen or eighty, the age-old enjoinders still apply: Know yourself, repent and renew yourself, renounce yourself, perfect yourself. Whatever the command, it holds from the cradle to the grave. It never gets any easier to save your soul.

Robert Frost emphasized this fact of life when answering the letter the *Amherst Spectator* wrote him on his sixtieth birthday. He put aside the whole idea of aging and wrote instead on the difficulty in saving one's soul. "Or if you dislike hearing your souls mentioned in a public meeting," he said, "say your 'decency' or your 'integrity.' "

Saving one's soul or decency or integrity is a never-ending task. Life is ever reduced to this: making one choice instead of another. At sixty, I am still living that day-by-day decision. Choice is still being presented, effort is being demanded. But in one way I am more fortunate than when I was younger. The pattern of my life is beginning to emerge. I have found what I do best, and now I can devote my time to doing it with all my might.

You seize control only by growing in truth and purpose and direction. For me, that began with my body —when I discovered the athlete resident in that blurred, out-of-focus body I was before I began running. Once I became conscious of the integrity of my body, I was on the way to that whole integrity of myself. I was running in the pursuit of those goals which have echoed down the centuries.

There is no book on this—no prescription on becoming a better person, the person you were meant to be, your own best friend. What has to be done is to live—to live fully and dangerously, to take chances. If there are rule, they are these: Use your body with intensity, play with utter absorption, accept pain and discipline and suffering as part of the game.

Pain is a large subject. I once spent an entire morning with a reporter in Seattle discussing where pain fit into the running life. He could not understand why pain was necessary. By the end of the morning, I wasn't sure myself.

In training, pain is something I usually avoid. I want the long, pleasant afternoon runs to be pain-free. Pain suppresses any creative mood, retards thinking and dams the stream of consciousness.

Yet there are days when pain is part of training. I challenge the hills; I do interval quarters. Sometimes, taking care so as not to pull a muscle, I sprint from one lamppost to another. And with each sprint, I strive to take as much pain as I can before I am forced to slow down.

It is not pain I seek. Pain is simply the symptom of lactic acid accumulating in my muscles, and I have to teach my body to handle lactic acid in races. You could as much say that I like lactic acid as suggest I like pain.

Pain is to be used. At times, it warns me I am doing something wrong. At other times, it signals I am doing right. If I am driving for the finish of a race and there is no pain, I know I have not yet pushed my body to its absolute limit. On the other hand, there is pain that commands to go this fast and no faster.

The runner is not a masochist. The runner does not enjoy pain. But between the runner and a personal best lies pain in quantity, both in training and in the race. And the pain, once endured, comes to have a value of its own. I do not seek suffering, but once it has been experienced I feel somehow the better for it.

There is only one answer to pain: Go out to meet it; plunge into it; grasp it as you would the nettle. There is always the chance that you will push through it into an area as calm and peaceful as the eye of the hurricane.

Pain has become my companion. For more than fifteen years, almost weekly and never less than twice a month, I have raced. I have gone where pain is and met it in races where pain is simply a constant like the wind or the rain or the footing.

At some point the final drive to the finish, the running is willed but no longer controlled. My body is running from memory. Running has become a reflex maintained only by a stubborn, unyielding, illogical determination not to stop.

The terrible tendency is to cheat on myself. Cheating in a race is making the effort tolerable. I am not here to make the race tolerable, or life either, for that matter.

Someone, probably a Russian, has written, "Go at once and seek suffering, accept it and bear it, and your heart will find comfort."

If you are looking for that suffering and that comfort, you can find them in running.

"The athlete," wrote one observer, "is a fanatic and an ascetic. A hard-driving, self-punishing, very special kind of human being utterly absorbed in a world that is out of this world." You will find no better example than Yukio Mishima. His psychological autobiography, *Sun and Steel*, traces his progress from a weak, frail individual with an inferiority complex about his physique to just such a person.

"In the summer of my 30th year," wrote Mishima, "I discovered the discipline of weightlifting." Thus began his search for himself through his body. From that beginning he went to boxing and then to Kendo, the modern version of samurai swordsmanship. The novelist, poet, actor became a superbly conditioned athlete. He developed not only the athlete's body but the athlete's mind and spirit as well. And made what he considered his most important discovery. Pain and the physical courage to deal with it.

Mishima brought a special perspective to the problem of pain. His was a new eye, a new ear, a new voice. He came from a world of art, not action; a world of fiction, not facts; a world of imagination, not flesh. In that world he had escaped pain in his own body. He had felt it in others; not himself. All that, he now saw, was a matter of coming in contact with shadows. "I lacked the physical courage," he wrote, "to seek suffering for myself, to take pain unto myself."

His encounter with his body changed that. First he felt pain; then he realized how important it was. Pain became an essential aspect of this new experience. "I perceive," he declared, "that the only physical proof of consciousness was suffering." Gradually, he said, there was born in him a tendency toward the physical acceptance of pain.

"During the past 10 years," he wrote, "I have learned strength; I have learned suffering, battle and self-conquest. I have learned courage to accept all with joy."

Being the writer he attempted to put this transformation and the causes of it into words. He tried taking the athletic life as it is lived and extracting the meat out of it. "Men by now have forgotten the profound inner struggle between consciousness and the body that exists in physical courage," he claimed.

"Consciousness (mind) is generally considered to be passive, and the active body to constitute the essence of all that is bold and daring; yet in the drama of physical courage, the roles are, in fact, reversed. The flesh beats a steady retreat into the function of self-defense, while it is the clear consciousness that sends the body into self-abandonment."

It is, of course, the athlete, that fanatic ascetic, who accepts pain and then charges past it. The athlete lives with pain. Pain is the guide on the ascent to an athlete's perfection. The barrier to that same attainment. Pain guards that final goal. It surrounds the athlete's personal summit.

Pain, therefore, is the only way to know when you are nearing your best, approaching your limits. Pain is the teacher. It gives true marks. It is the true measure. And in following pain the athlete is following human nature. Pain is part of the ascetic instinct. We place no value on anything we get cheaply, and rightly so; the more effort, the more discomfort, the more hardship, the happier we are. When we think on it, asceticism seems quite the best way to live one's life. William James thought so. Now a modern philosopher seems to agree with him.

"The ascetic impulse," wrote William Barrett in *The Illusion of Technique,* "is much stronger than we think and forms a not inconsiderable part of the sense of discipline without which life would cease to have meaning.

"The frenzies of asceticism, which may seem mere aberration and abnormality to our minds, are in fact the inevitable means by which the human animal is driven to give meaning to his existence. We create by denying ourselves. So long as we drive ourselves in the toil of some discipline, we cannot believe that our life is meaningless."

So pain puts the seal on consciousness, gives meaning to life and at the same time refutes Descartes: "The body is but a fiction of my mind." Pain makes us answer affirmatively to Maslow's question, "What is one truly if not first and foremost one's body, one's constitution, one's own functioning?"

No athlete thinks otherwise. When I began running and discovered my body, I also discovered pain. It was there in every race. At the mile mark if I had chosen my pace carefully. Much sooner if I had not. And in training it was anywhere I chose. At the crest of every hill. Or the space between two telephone poles. Whenever I pushed myself enough I could fill my body with pain. At any given moment I could have a collision with my limits.

I too learned that pain defined my "I." I began to see the Self, divided then whole. Pain revealed what the Will is. Not determination about the future. Not a decision about what is to be done. Will is the acceptance of the Now, the painful, suffering, exhausting present in which I now exist.

The race told me most. It is life intensified. The possible and the impossible not yet purely defined. The race is a fierce struggle in which I am my own competitor. "If you want to win a race," Bill Rodgers has said, "you have to go a little berserk." It is the best advice I have ever heard.

If you want to win anything, a race, your self, your

life, you have to go a little berserk. If you want to make a leap in consciousness, or personal growth, or self-esteem, you have to go a little berserk. You have to have a new vision. You have to become utterly absorbed in another world, in what James called a new and greater reality. Where you exist as your true and perfect self, the once and future king.

When I am in pain and hating it, I remember what Emerson said: "What would you have; quoth God; Take what you want and pay for it." When the prize is the self, the payment is pain.

I am not at all sure I am a fanatic, ascetic, hard-driving, self-punishing person, but I am ready to meet that price.

One summer I had a lingering leg injury and could not run for about two weeks. I swam instead. Long distance in the ocean. Interval sprints in the pool.

I would do the length of the pool, about fifty yards, at close to top speed. Then climb out, walk back and do it again. Fifty yards swimming is roughly equal to 200 yards running on the track. An all-out fifty yards in the water takes just as much out of me, and possibly a little more since I am a runner, as a 220-yard sprint.

The sensations are much the same. With each one there is a gradual buildup of pain. Discomfort first, then the leaden ache in the arms and legs, finally the whole body screaming. And each successive interval raises the base line of that pain a notch or two higher.

One day I was in the final stages of such a workout, feeling and, apparently, showing the ordeal I was putting myself through. A woman who had been watching came up to me.

"Dr. Sheehan," she said, "I hope you are writing all this down somewhere."

She found the entire episode incomprehensible. Yet at the same time she realized that there must be something here that had value. There must be something worth all this effort and suffering.

There are, of course, physiological reasons for running interval sprints. These sharpening techniques are the final preparation for my assaults on my best times at almost any distance. Invervals raise my anaerobic threshold. They enable me to cruise at a higher speed. Interval quarters done once a week will improve my times noticeably within a month.

But such inducements are not what keep me doing just one more, and then another, and another, testing myself again and again. The physiological formula doesn't require those final two or three. The more painful they become, the less need to do them. So why do I continue? What is actually happening when I do these interval workouts?

As I see it, interval training is as much for the will as it is for the body. I am getting my will ready for the race. I am, in fact, running the race in advance. I am trying to reach that interval quarter which will feel exactly the same as the last lap of a race. And then be able to deal with it mentally as well as physically.

In interval quarters the will is paramount. The will makes me finish one interval. It calls up the energies to do another. William James, who was a student of the energies of man, wrote much on this. He was vitally interested in how we could mobilize the forces which we contain deep within us.

For James this effort was the measure of man.

"Effort," he wrote, "is the one strictly underived and original contribution we make to this world." Everything else is given to us. Health, strength, talent, abilities of all sorts, whether spiritual or mental or physical. Effort is the only element we can add. "He alone is happy," James wrote, "who has will. The rest are zeroes. He uses, they are used."

Otto Rank, who was Freud's protégé, also wrote extensively on the same subject. Like James, he was concerned with the heroic and the exuberances of man. For him as well, the will was all. The will was our only real resource in dealing with life, which Rank viewed as an irrational situation from which there was no escape. We have to deal with the fact that we have been given this will to immortality, despite the reality that we must die.

We all respond to this paradox in our own way. We ignore it, explain it away, find security in belief in the hereafter, or deal with it at a personal level. This last, said Rank, depended on the will. A person, he thought, experiences his individuality in terms of his will. His personal existence is identical to his capacity to express his will in this world.

I know of few better ways to reach this primitive level where will and effort combine than interval quarters. The answer to life's question becomes simply, yes or no. There is no place for explanations, qualifications, excuses. Will I or will I not continue until I know this is truly the last lap?

I remember one time running interval quarters in a high school stadium during football practice. There were fifty or more football players on the field going through drills. They took no notice of me as I did one repeat quarter after another. That day as always the laps gradually became more and more difficult. After each successive interval my distress became more obvious. The gasping more noticeable. The groaning a little louder.

Finally I collapsed on the grass, knowing there was only one more quarter in me and then only if I could force myself to do it.

I lay there for the longest time. The two minutes had almost expired when I finally raised myself, got to my hands and knees. Then I noticed that practice had stopped and they were watching me, curious to see what I would do. It was as if I were an animal hit at long range and they were waiting to see if I would get up and trot off into the woods.

Then I did get up and started jogging slowly to the starting line. Behind me I could hear this cheer ringing, and then someone shouting, "Way to go, Doc."

I will not last forever, but I am damn well going to know I have been here. That day, so did they.

There is a tendency these days to see mental pressure as something to be avoided. We view mental health as a state in which we are free from the feeling that there is something wrong with us; free from the need to become more and more; free from the tension between what we are and what we should be. Mental health, we are led to believe, is to be once and for all free from pressure.

Actually, it is quite the opposite. Mental health comes with the ability to live with these feelings, these needs, these tensions. These pressures are as essential as they are unavoidable. They are our way to salvation.

It is, appropriately, a salvation that requires religion. William James pointed this out in his *Gospel of Relaxation*. Religion, he stated, was the sovereign remedy for worry. The really religious person, he said, is unshakable and calmly ready for any duty the day might bring forth.

We common folk know this. There is an expression we use about people "getting religion." We apply it when people finally realize their sport or study or project requires hard work and discipline and dedication, and that it is likely to be filled with failures and false starts. Yet knowing this, they discover the will to decide, and the strength and energy and faith to persevere. They know you've gotta believe.

Religion generates the same attitude as play: the certainty that whatever happens, things will be all right; that there is no final defeat in this world, and within the rules and the rituals we can be as free and inventive as we please.

Play in a sense anticipates religion. It takes us past our basic needs, beyond being fed and housed and kept warm. Play can give us self-knowledge, although in the process we may get cold and wet and go without food. Play is also a theater of heroism. In play, we become capable of facing what must be faced, of enduring what must be endured and somehow coming through in the end.

William Faulkner, in accepting the Nobel Prize for Literature, said, "man will not merely endure: he will prevail. He is immortal, not because he alone among creatures has an inexhaustible voice, but because he has a soul, a spirit capable of compassion and sacrifice and endurance."

That is my project—that this person, however weak, however cowardly, however fearful, however anxious, should somehow not only endure, but prevail. But first, I gotta believe.

"What strikes me about this whole scene," said my friend who is a playwright, "is how gentle everyone is." We were standing at the finish of the Berkshires Masters Ten-Kilometer Run watching the runners stream by. Beyond the grass homestretch on the soccer field was a small grandstand packed with cheering friends and families. Now and then the applause would rise to another peak as a woman or older man dashed the final yards to the finish.

Only moments before I had come through that finish line wrapped in that silent struggle with myself, deep in the private torture that occurs in the last stages of a race. I had gone through those final six or seven minutes where just maintaining my pace is a notable act of courage. I had heard the same applause. Gotten my time and number. Shook hands, touched others, been embraced. And now stood filled with those wonderful sentiments that fill my soul after a race.

And as I looked into myself and looked at those around me, I realized my friend was right. Gentle was the way to describe it. Gentle and perhaps one word more. Peaceful. A poet friend of mine had used the word. She had never, she told me, seen a face more filled with peace than mine after a race.

The peace is a positive quality. It is not merely the absence of stress or strife or conflict. It is a peace that is active. A peace that is strong. It is a peace that has certainty. A peace that tells me that I am good and holy and complete.

It is also a peace that is rare. All other acts carry within them a counterreaction. There is the depression that follows exultation. The sadness that comes after ecstasy. Not so with the race and the peace that follows. This peace is the fruit of the race. Something born of that suffering, that testing, that exhibition of character, that attainment of class.

And with it comes the relaxation, the elimination of desires, the end of craving, the death of ambition. For a time pettiness and the lesser appetites and all the meanness are wiped out. I have put on the new man.

Earlier I had been more concerned with records and performance. While I was warming up a runner came up to me and said, "You'll set a new record, for sure." I thought not. It was my third race in a week and within that week I had been forced to slow to a walk at the three-mile mark in a training run because of fatigue.

As I had jogged up and down the soccer field where

the race was to start and finish, I felt my thighs rubbing together, a sure sign of exhaustion. I stopped thinking then about records and concentrated on the thought of doing my best. I was going to do poorly, I knew, but whatever it was it must be my best.

I need not have worried.

It turned out to be one of those days when everything went well. It was an easy out-and-back course with no hills. The weather did its part; the day was one of those beautiful, dry, clear days in New England, the sky an uninterrupted blue.

Right from the start I felt good and began to feel even better after the first mile. On the way back I felt so strong it was a matter of controlling my speed lest I sprint the entire last three miles. I had my age group won and was beginning to think about the record.

The sequence was much like one a psychiatrist-runner had outlined in a letter to me, describing a half-marathon. "As I started the run," he wrote, "I recalled the lines from Wordsworth's 'Happy Warrior.' By the time I had reached halfway I thought of Kipling's 'If.' By the ninth mile I began praying. That carried me until close to the finish, when simple physiology became dominant."

I was reliving that experience along with everyone else in the race. The first half was the Happy Warrior, "playing in the many games of life the one where what he dost most value must be won." Then as I neared the last few miles it became Kipling and the task of "filling every minute with sixty seconds of distance run."

By this time I had the record in hand, but I could not back off. It was no longer my record, it was everybody's record. I was no longer running for myself. I was running for the 430 people in this race and every runner who would look at what a sixty-year-old had done and feel proud. Despite the pain I had to break that record by the greatest margin possible.

Then as I searched desperately up ahead for the final turn into the soccer field, it was prayer. The usual prayer of the runner: "Let this cup pass." In the end, of course, it was the body gradually reducing its function, but the will refusing to accept anything but collapse. Trying, in fact, to make the finish and the collapse coincide.

Out of that common experience came the scene that was unfolding before us. This spontaneous meeting of bodies and souls as runner after runner came from that common ordeal. There is no purer embrace, someone once wrote, that than of the vanquished and the victor on the battlefield.

Here was its equivalent, except there was no vanquished. All of us were victors. All of us had gone through levels of effort, levels of pain and hence levels of performance which were, by standards of our everyday existence, superhuman. All of us were record breakers. We embraced as equals.

The race is the key. The race and everything that happens in it. Mostly that is pain. Pain that is in time and therefore never ending. Pain that is the negative eternity Hegel wrote about. And because I have lived with this pain and accepted it and offered it for all my fellow runners I have gained this peace. The peace that is Hegel's positive eternity. The peace that is outside of time and therefore unending.

The last finisher was in and it was time for the food and the awards. We stood in line for chowder and beans and franks and got our soda and beer. Then we sat at long tables eating and drinking and exchanging stories of the race we had just run and others we could remember.

And a gentle peace filled that Sunday afternoon in the Berkshires in New England.

11

The Stress

Stress is a necessity. We must not avoid it. If not present, we must seek it out. This is especially true in a matter of physical stress, which has become voluntary.

We are no longer obliged to use our bodies. So physical stress must be sought and accepted, applied and endured if we are to become fit. And further, our stress must be of sufficient intensity and our rest periods of adequate duration to build us up rather than tear us down.

What each of us must do, it seems to me, is become an athlete: pick our sport, decide on our event, undergo training, learn technique. No matter that we are the worst in the world at what we do. We must do it. Only in that way will we bridge the gap between what we were born to be and what we are now.

The effect of athletic training, the application of measured amounts of stress separated by suitable periods of recuperation, is easily seen. The difference between the me who began running almost two decades ago and the me who runs thirty miles a week now is the difference between two worlds.

In the first, I did no more than exist. I was able to do what I did for a living and very little more. I fell asleep regularly before the TV set at night. Whatever I did followed the path of least resistance. Anything physical required a push. I was, in a word, a vegetable. Technically, however, I was in good health. I had no active disease. There was no disability that kept me from my daily rounds. What I did not have was true health, zest, enthusiasm, an enjoyment of living. I did not have the capacity to live twenty-four hours a day with the ease and grace and endurance appropriate to the human animal.

Now, I enjoy those things the exercise physiologists promise anyone who would become an athlete—the fruits they guarantee to anyone who would give up the distractions of an affluent society, the rewards for returning to the trials and hardships of another day, the benefits available to those who eat only when hungry and sit only when legitimately tired.

Your heart, the experts say, will become larger and more efficient. You will have a slower pulse and a higher work capacity. Your vital capacity will also increase, as will your ability to take in oxygen and get rid of carbon dioxide. Further, your capillaries will increase and so will your blood volume. The net effect of these changes will be better function of the body at every level down to the tiniest cell. If you train, the scientists say, you will become normal, which is to say the best there is.

I confirmed for myself the claims the researchers made. I underwent a series of tests in a Midwestern medical school. Everything they said would happen did. My fitness scores would be considered excellent for someone thirty years my junior. My endurance capacity was that of a man near his prime.

My first thought was that I was a superior being. My physiologist friend, however, said no. My oxygen intake, he said, was almost all due to a training effect. I was just an ordinary sixty-year-old using stress to the limit and reaping the rewards. He viewed my results as nothing special—just what could be expected from the common, garden-variety human body when stressed correctly.

There are some who think as I once did that athletes are extraordinary people, that athletes are somehow different both physically and psychologically from non-athletes. If so, it is only because the non-athlete has not yet discovered the joys of stress, not yet found the delightful and engrossing and fulfilling process of becoming the person he is.

Everyone is an athlete. The only difference is that some of us are in training, and some are not.

It occurred to me while running that there must be an equivalent training program for the mind. "A sound mind in a sound body" implies that physical and psychological fitness must proceed from the same principles, in fact from the same source.

The basis of the sound body is, of course, stress—stress applied in measured and constantly increasing quantities with suitable intervals of time between to allow the body to adapt. What makes this process work, however, is play. What makes us fit must be sport, or we won't participate. What makes us healthy must come from a self-renewing inner compulsion, or we won't persist in it. What makes us athletes must become an essential part of our day, or our bodies will rebel against it.

If play is the answer to our physical life, should not play be the answer to our psychological life as well? Does not our mental health depend upon play as surely as our physical health does? Will not the play that made us athletes also make us saints?

I put it to you that it does. There is no question in my mind that the best way to handle psychological stress is play. The surest way to develop a sound mind is through humor. How better, then, to deal with stress than with humor?

Humor allows us to tolerate the intolerable, to accept the unacceptable, to bear the unbearable, even to understand the incomprehensible. Humor gives us the capacity to live with ambiguity, the courage to take chances, the strength to go forward without solutions.

What humor does is reduce life to the game that it is. It allows us to take a long look at the real world and all that is evil about us, yet to know that it is somehow part of the plan. Only a sense of humor can help each of us face those great unanswerable questions: Why was I born? Why am I here? Why must I die? What must I do to make my life a triumph?

Long before stress had become our major problem, decades before those who doctor our physical and social ills had recognized its importance, almost a century before authors and publishers had found it to be a profitable and inexhaustible subject, William James had made it a central theme of his lectures.

James was a Boston Brahmin—an aristocrat by birth, position and intellect. He had known stress first-hand. He had been exposed to what must be our greatest danger—security. His initial response had been to comtemplate suicide. Rejecting that, he had gone on to develop his own universe. It was a world filled with uncertainty, choice, hypothesis, novelty and possibility. It was an incomplete world, a world in the making, in which man was the most important ingredient. It was a world which demanded no less than his best, a world which required the strenuous life, and was filled with challenge and stress.

In 1900, when James was writing, life was not easy except for the privileged few. Over one third of Americans were farmers. Two thirds of the remainder had manual jobs requiring considerable physical effort. Even the white-collar workers did a considerable amount of walking during the long hours of their work week.

Now, of course, all is changed. Technology has freed all but 3 percent of us from the farms. It has reduced and in most cases removed the manual labor of almost half of the work force still in service jobs. The result is that only about 5 percent of Americans are at jobs that keep them physically fit. The rest of us are gradually succumbing to this new leisure economy. The privileged few have become the privileged many. The common man has become an aristocrat.

Now, challenge and insecurity must be sought. They are not thrust upon us. We have to go back to fundamentals. We need to feel danger, chase after conflict, seek stress. Our aim is "a sound mind in a sound body." Stress is simply the resistance we encounter in seeking that health for our body and truth for our soul.

James said all that at the turn of the century. Every one of us, he thought, needs muscular vigor not to fight the old heavy battles with nature, but to furnish a background of sanity and serenity and cheerfulness to life.

Today, only the athlete knows that feeling. Only the athlete feels the inner peace and confidence that James said wells up from every part of the body of the well-trained human being. James, the intellectual and aristocrat, saw clearly the importance of the body. He knew it was the substrate upon which every other value, mental or spiritual, must take root.

In his commencement address to the women graduates of the Boston Normal School of Gymnastics, William James spoke of what he termed the most generally useful precept in one's self-discipline. It was the rule that bid us pay primary attention to what we do and express, and not care too much for what we feel. Action and feeling go together, James declared, and by regulating the action which is under the direct control of the will we can indirectly control the feeling which is not.

He said we should act cheerful, and act as if we were brave, and force ourselves to say genial things. Then, we would indeed be cheerful and brave and even feel kindly toward those who might annoy us. Whatever stress we were faced with, we could *will* the needed action and hope that our feelings would follow.

This necessity of having the correct attitude has been emphasized recently by the world's expert on stress, Dr. Hans Selye. The way to handle stress, he said, involves taking a different attitude toward the various events of our life.

"Adopting the right attitude," he said, "can convert a negative stress into a positive stress." (For this positive stress, he has coined the term *eustress*, implying good effects.)

The word "attitude" is apt, for it implies more than a point of view, although that in itself is terribly important. In a sense, my attitude is no less than my view of the universe; how I am in the world and what I intend to do about it.

What James and Selye are championing is that we take this word in its positive meaning—that we come, as the athletes say, to play. Such an attitude sees the world as good, and it will somehow be the better for me living in it. It is the conviction that life is a game and that I am a real part of it; I have a role to play. It is the trust that whatever happens, I need have no apprehension about the outcome.

When I see life that way, as the game it is, I am in a position to accept stress. In sport, stress is welcomed. The worse the going is, the better. Obstacles, hardships, the most terrible of conditions only make the game more exciting and rewarding. There is no thrill in an easy win or beating someone weaker. Competition is welcomed because it brings out the best in me.

Do not for a minute think play is not serious. Play is more serious and demanding than anything else I will do. Play is a true measure of how I value myself and what I am willing to do to become the person I am.

Plato saw this. "Life," he said, "must be lived as play—playing certain games, singing and dancing. Then will man propitiate the gods, defend himself against his enemies and win the contest."

12

The Rest

My friend Tom Osler, who is an ultra-marathoner and teaches math at a state college, says that depressions are a part of life. The runner, he says, must expect them—even welcome them. They are just as normal, just as inevitable, just as important and just as necessary as the happy times.

I am inclined to agree. Periodically, no matter how I try to avoid it, I run myself into a growing inner discontent. Every six months or so, I develop the feeling that every task is too difficult and little worth the effort anyway.

My running suffers most. In fact, it is the first indication that things are amiss. I no longer look forward to my daily run. And should I ignore this lack of zest and run anyway, I tire easily and don't enjoy it. But the running and this loss of enjoyment are only part of it. My moods, my concentration, my attitude toward myself and others are all affected. Instead of battling anoxia and lactic acid and muscles depleted of sugar, I am in hand-to-hand combat with dejection and dependency, with rejection and self-pity, with guilt and loneliness.

Such periods are inescapable. Ecclesiastes was right; there is a time for everything. Human nature frowns on prudence. It demands that we maximize ourselves, do whatever we do with all our might. Predictably, this means periodic exhaustion, periodic failure, periodic depression and, happily, periodic re-evaluation.

"The athlete in training is a sleepy creature," wrote Plato in *The Republic*. "Haven't you noticed how they sleep most of the time and how the slightest deviation from their routine leads to serious illness?"

Athletes have not changed since the time of the ancient Greeks. We still are people who require much sleep and many naps. We still get ill whenever our routine is changed. But mainly we are still distinguished by our almost total collapse when we overtrain. This is probably as it should be. The penalty should fit the crime. To the Greeks, pride was the greatest sin. And what is training but pride?

When I train, I am pushing myself to the absolute limit. I am testing the furthermost reaches of my body's integrity. I am trying to go beyond anything I have done before. I am seeking the breaking point of my physiology. Should I pass that limit, I should get more than a slap on the wrist. I should get appropriate punishment, some clear signal that I have exceeded my capacities. And I do. It is called "staleness" and consists of a variety of symptoms which add up to remind me that I am mortal.

When I get stale, I accept this reminder of my finitude. I relax and vegetate. I eat and sleep and nap. Instead of running an hour a day, I take a nap for an hour a day. This routine usually proves to be sufficient penance, and in a week or ten days I am back running at a suitably lower level.

However, there are runners who find that eating and sleeping and napping are not enough. For them, the fatigue persists, the depression goes on, the zest will not return, the curse will not lift. For these runners, days become weeks and weeks, months—and still running is a chore, and performance is never quite the same as before. They are in the dark night of the soul.

Brendan Foster, a world-record-holder from Britain, once described a distance runner as a person who went to bed tired at night and got out of bed even more tired in the morning. I think he was wrong. That is the description of a distance runner headed for trouble. When that state occurs, it is time for rest and reassessment.

Plato said we needed a more sophisticated form of training. It is time we heeded his advice.

In running, as with everything in life, there can be too much of a good thing—too much training but especially too much racing. It is extremely hard to resist the excitement and challenge of a race. So the runner can become overraced just as the tennis player is overtennised and the golfer is overgolfed.

My mail is filled with letters about this phenomenon: high school seniors who have never achieved their sophomore promise, college runners now unable to get back to what they did in high school, club runners who are getting worse instead of better, runners everywhere wondering why their bodies are breaking down.

It is a mystery, this state of staleness—the heavy legs, the rapid pulse, the frequent colds, the loss of zest, the poor performances. There is no specific test that can pin it down. Nor is there any test that will warn me when I have reached my peak, and the next race or hard workout will send me over the cliff into a state of fatigue and depression.

That knowledge is just what we need. The runner who is in peak condition is only a razor's edge from catastrophe. A personal best time is, to be sure, an occasion for joy and celebration, but it should also make the runner quite cautious about trying to better the performance immediately. I have come to the conclusion that the proper response to running an outstanding race is to take a week off to savor it.

Intelligent runners tend to do that. In fact, the winner of one fifty-six-mile Comrades run in South Africa took *six weeks* off before resuming training. Few of us, however, have that common sense. Few of us read our bodies that well. A great race, we are inclined to think, is evidence of an even greater race inside. With a little more speedwork and some time on the hills, who knows what marvelous things can happen? The marvelous things, however, often turn out to be those dismal complaints.

The clearest warning of impending staleness is a bad race. Nine times out of ten, this slump means the runner is overtrained, but the impulse is to go out and train harder. That only digs the pit deeper. The proper approach to this all-too-human problem is to recognize the wisdom of Ecclesiastes, which says there is a time for everything. There is a time to race, a time not to race. This is a time to be elated, a time to be depressed. There is a time to be king of your hill, a time to be at the bottom of the heap. There is a time to train, a time to nap.

When you restore the Biblical rhythm to your days, you will be able to accept staleness. And when you do, it will disappear.

When William Jones spoke on "The Gospel of Relaxation" to the women graduates of the Boston Normal School of Gymnastics, his theme was the vital necessity of the fit and relaxed body to mental health.

Fitness comes first, of course. In saying this, James was echoing the Greeks. In their society, gymnastics was a crucial component of each citizen's life. So James was delighted to address these women athletes. Already, he declared, they had gained that general sense of security and readiness for anything that might turn up. They had discovered, he was sure, the benefits of energy and initiative and independence. But to make the most of these new-found capabilities, they must also learn, he said, to relax.

No statement would be more in character. James was one of the originators of the James-Lange theory of emotions. He believed that emotions begin in the body, not in the mind. We become excited or aggravated or sad or tense *after* our bodies become excited or aggravated or sad or tense, not before. The overtense, excited body, therefore, keeps us in an overtense, excited state of mind.

"It is not the nature of our work that accounts for our breakdowns," he told the graduates, "but those absurd feelings of hurry, of not having time, that breathlessness and tension, that solicitude for results, and that lack of harmony and ease by which the work is accompanied."

This analysis is echoed in some current views on stress. Dr. Meyer Friedman has described the type-A behavior of coronary patients in almost identical terms. "Such behavior," says Friedman, "is an action-emotion complex exhibited by individuals engaged in an incessant struggle to achieve more and more in less and less time."

Friedman sees such behavior as accelerating certain components of the autonomic nervous system, thus causing cardiac damage. These victims of the "hurry sickness" are not deterred by warnings of another heart attack. They must be shown, says Friedman, that they are cheating themselves—that in being totally absorbed in obtaining the things worth *having* they have stopped doing the things worth *doing*.

The Greeks told us that. James told us that. Now, Dr. Friedman is telling us that. Perhaps we ought to listen.

Running is my relaxation technique. When I run, I relax. When I run, I meditate. Instead of becoming immobile and closing my eyes and repeating my word, I take the opposite course. I run and open my eyes and move into inaccessible areas of my mind and soul.

Movement is the key. Movement is the mantra that opens up my mind. It is the rhythm that leads to relaxation. The need for movement is basic to our nature, to our physical and mental health. Our well-being, our adaptation to stress literally depend upon moving about.

Nietzsche told us, "Never trust an idea you come upon sitting down."

And Thoreau, whose inspiration came with walking, said, "Methinks that the moment my legs begin to move, my thoughts begin to flow."

Compared to running, other relaxation techniques seem to me like so much first aid. I use them for rest, recovery and restoration of energy. But motion is vital. Contemplating my navel is of no use unless both I and my navel are in movement. Nor does descending into the subconscious make sense unless I am going to look around when I get there.

Running brings everything together. What running does is increase my receptivity, raise my consciousness, heighten my perception. What follows is simply a temporary stay against chaos, a brief glimpse of beauty or perfection that helps me to face the ever-present stress and uncertainties of my life.

When I run, I know as you do that nothing is ever settled. There will be no answers until there is no need for them. We live in an open-ended world. There are, as William James said, no conclusions.

In ways I only dimly understand, running encourages me to live with my uncertainties. It enables me to view the future not as ominous but full of promise. Indeed, there are days I feel as if I was, am and ever shall be—which is about as relaxed as you can get.

13

The Results

I had come to Phoenix to address the top employees of a giant conglomerate at their annual business meeting. The pattern of these get-togethers is familiar. First, everyone is congratulated for a successful year. Then, they are told that much more is expected of them in the next twelve months. They did great, but they must do better.

The scenario reminds me of a story about Vince Lombardi when he was coaching Green Bay. The Packers had won this day and were filing out of the stadium through a cheering crowd of spectators. One of the fans leaned over and yelled to Jim Taylor, the hard-hitting fullback, something about playing a great game.

Taylor turned to him and said, "By the time Lombardi gets through with us in the locker room, we'll think we lost this game."

What football players learned under Lombardi and what employees learn at annual meetings is that the game is never over, the contest never ends. The company is not interested in past successes. It is not interested in retirement and Florida condominiums. It is terribly and vitally interested in performance, the day-to-day doing of routine things well and ordinary things better.

This meeting was no exception. The president spoke about growth. Their company, he said, had grown enormously and competently through the acquisition of other companies. Now, that period was over. They would no longer take over other companies. From now on, their growth would be internal, not external.

This growth, he went on, must of necessity come from their own resources. It could not be someone else's strength, someone else's assets, someone else's know-how, someone else's initiative. And it would have to be a true growth, not some bookkeeping sleight-of-hand.

Such a program, he concluded, would leave no room for complacency. They could not rest on what they had done. This was not the time to hunker down and be content with where they were. He was sure, however, they would be up to it. It took him about an hour to give them the bad news.

As I sat there, I thought to myself, he is giving my speech. He is talking about corporate fitness in the way I was going to talk about individual fitness. The individual also comes to a time where growth must be internal.

When I rose to speak, I told them the good news. The company would grow, and they would grow with it. First, they had to see where they were, then they could see where they were going. We are much like the corporation. We rely on external aids rather than organic growth. We, too, use some tricky bookkeeping to prove that we are as good as we ever were. We, too, reach a time when we must grow out of our own resources—a growth that is a day-to-day progress and, simultaneously, the building up of new energy, a new vision, a new person.

I was not there, I told them, to sell fitness on the basis of longevity but on performance, not because it reduced risk factors but because it contributed to growth. I could see, I told them, that a vibrant, growing corporation must have vibrant, growing employees. So corporate growth depends upon individual growth; corporate performance rests upon individual performance, and the fitness of the corporation hinges upon the fitness of the individual personnel.

In parting, I told them about a friend of mine who had been a swimmer in college. When he joined this company, he started swimming during his lunch hour so he would outlive all the other executives. In the process, however, he outworked them, outthought them and outcreated them. He outdid them in everything connected with his job. When he finally came out of that pool, he was the president.

There came a time last year when I was fed up with conducting medical clinics for runners. That weekend, as so often in the past, I was on a program with

Dr. David Costill. My role was to discuss injuries. His was to show how the exercise physiologist could help the runner.

When I saw Dave, I told him, "There must be something better we can do with our time than saying the same old things one meeting after another."

Dave looked at me, smiled and said, "George, they're hungry out there."

He's right. They are hungry. Distance running is more than a sport. It is a way of life. And the running life requires more and more knowledge of the workings of the human body. Distance runners are hungry for any information they can get. I should not need to be reminded of that. Runners ask more questions than a three-year-old. Their questions are just as basic and just as difficult. I'm as hungry as the next one—and just as likely to be at Dave Costill's lecture, taking notes.

Dave has the last word on physiology for me. He is one of the few scientists I have been associated with who has a complete grasp of his subject. When Dave says, "I don't know," I realize nobody knows. Most runners feel the same. For us, Costill has become the Answer Man.

Costill also is that rare academic individual—the exceptional scientist who is also an exceptional teacher. When he takes his six feet, one inch, 162-pound frame up to the podium, he commands a quality of attention you rarely find in school. People who last attended classes only under duress vie for front-row seats. Students who never were true students can be seen busily checking their notes. Others who cut more classes than they attend eagerly follow Costill's intricate and sophisticated outlines of body functions.

Costill didn't come to this level of acceptance by accident. He has gilt-edged credentials as an exercise physiologist. If there were an exercise physiology hall of fame, he would make it on the first ballot. The literature is filled with significant work that has come out of his laboratory at Ball State University in Muncie, Indiana.

His standing with his colleagues is indicated by his election as president of the American College of Sports Medicine and his recent medal for the application of science to sport. This regard reflects not only his professional competence but his modesty as well. He is the academic counterpart of Bill Rodgers. He is so unself-conscious about his achievements and takes them so lightly, you begin to wonder whether this relaxed person in front of you is really the number one running physiologist in the country, if not the world.

When I first met Dave, I was overwhelmed by the range and depth of his knowledge. He moved around the Krebs Cycle, for instance, like I moved around my own home. So for some time I restricted my conversation to "yes," "no" and "Where's the bathroom?" It wasn't long, however, before I discovered that like most "biggies" (as he calls those he admires) Dave was more concerned about his own ignorance than mine. He treats everyone as another searcher after truth with something to contribute.

There is another reason why we distance runners admire Costill and flock to hear him. What he offers is practical. It works. We can take it out the next day and use it. In this sense he is a throwback to the clinical professors I had in medical school. Unlike the academics, these men were actually in the day-to-day practice of medicine. What they taught could be applied to the next patient.

Costill is a clinical exercise physiologist. When he performs a biopsy on a muscle, it is a runner's muscle. When he studies the emptying of a stomach, it is a runner's stomach. When he tests a replacement solution's effect on rectal temperature, it is a runner's rectal temperature.

And the truth is that Dave Costill is as hungry to teach as we runners are hungry to learn. Perhaps that is why Dave and I still go around the country giving clinics, saying the same things time and again. It isn't often that you face students as eager to be taught as you are to teach.

For almost as many years as I have been writing, I have been making periodic phone calls to Joe Henderson to tell him I am through, washed up; I will never again write anything worth reading. And for just as many years, he has reassured me that all will be well. He has reminded me that I have passed innumerable such crises before, and this one too shall pass.

I go through the ritual because Joe is the only person I trust when it comes to writing about running. If I have one sentence, even one word, that is weak or exaggerated or untrue, he will catch it immediately. If the writing is a fraction off-key, a hair out of tune, his eye and ear will detect it. When it comes to running-writing, Joe has perfect pitch. So if I write anything that passes his editorial scrutiny, I know I need not care about anyone else's opinion.

When I look for the truth about running, I read Joe Henderson and those writers who have passed his editorial standards. What he demands is not sincerity alone; every runner-writer seems to have that quality. It is not enough to want to tell the truth; the revelation has to go deeper and use just the right words in doing it. What Joe asks for is veracity, which is a product of sincerity, plus discipline, hard work and the desire to use yourself up completely. Veracity has a clarity that sincerity can only strive for.

Joe brings that clarity to his writing. He is a deceptively simple writer who makes it look easy. His instinct and intuition about the running experience give him complete control, complete confidence. As you read his work, this control becomes evident. There is the leaving unsaid of things that need not be said, the avoidance of pretense about things he doesn't know.

What he knows is enough. Henderson once referred to running as a thinking person's sport. Subsequent events have proven him correct. Running has attracted and continues to attract individuals of all temperaments, but none more strongly than those who live in the mind.

Joe is of similar bent. What he felt was felt by those of us coming after him. What he saw we were led to see. What delighted him eventually delighted us as well. Reading him confirmed our own experience and allowed us to anticipate what would happen next.

During his years as its editor, *Runner's World Magazine* took on the unique character it still has. It became a magazine for the participant, not the spectator; a journal for those who would be heroes rather than hero-worshippers. It became a monthly written by and for the runners themselves. You had a voice in it as long as you told the truth about running.

Joe Henderson is now getting the recognition he deserves, but this will never change him. He is the most modest writer I have ever met, the gentlest and most understanding editor. It is sufficient reward to him that he has a talent, and a passion and an opportunity to use it.

What he is uncompromising about is his writing time. He writes as he runs, seven days every week. He gave up editing the magazine when it began to cut into this time. He now writes and edits other runner-writers' books in his small workshop on the Monterey Peninsula of California. His books are the product of that daily writing and running, those excursions into his inner and outer worlds.

Joe's book have encouraged every runner to think of him as a friend. I sometimes think of him as more than that, more like a twin. Once, for instance, I called him to suggest an outline for a brochure we had planned.

"I've already written it that way," he told me.

I think of my relationship with Joe as being unique, but I'm sure it isn't. Others also see him as their alter ego—the me without my faults, the best I could be. Others also call him and get reassurance that all is well. Others also have that faith in his ability to determine what is first-rate and what is ordinary, and find in his approval an unshakeable confidence in themselves and their writing.

Joe Henderson, in his quiet way, has given us and our sport credibility. His writings have validated the running experience. But he has also demonstrated an even more important truth: Once you have decided that winning isn't everything, you become a winner.

The three of us—my friend Mel, who is also my agent, myself and the man from the beer company— were sitting in the upstairs lounge of an east side athletic club. It was one of those places where you have to wear a jacket and tie. Mine, which matched neither each other nor the rest of my clothes, I had borrowed from the man who checked the coats. But it was the talk that made me more uncomfortable than the clothes.

The beer man had flown in from Missouri to induce me to write a brochure on running. He had read, he said, that I drank beer during races and had written to this effect in my column. I had, in fact, recommended beer as an excellent source of both fluid and energy. And now, with my help, this company would like to put out a pamphlet on running which contained some favorable reference to beer—not their beer, any beer.

The man was very persuasive. He said his company believes in sports, sports are good for America, and what's good for America is good for his company. The interest in running is just the kind of an activity the company wants to aid and be associated with.

So do a lot of companies, I thought. Running has

become a major industry. Shoes, clothes and races are bringing business and advertising into the running scene. That was the rub. It appeared that everyone was in it for the money—including me.

For a dozen or more years, I had written because I had wanted to. I was doing something I would have done for nothing. I had discovered a job that wasn't work. And, in fact, I was getting almost nothing to do it—a ten-spot a week from the newspaper, and until a few years ago not even postage for conducting a question-and-answer service and column for the magazine. I never complained; I knew that I would have paid to have it printed.

Now, the money was coming in like it did at Sutter's Mill. Everyone wanted to pay me for something—to endorse, recommend, wear, attend, speak, write—you name it. It was no longer a question of counting the money. It had to be weighed.

The time had come to get my bearings, to set rules and follow them. There is nothing wrong with money. "I don't actually like money," Joe Louis said, "but it does ease the nerves." The idea is not to get nervous about making it, not to see it as an end in itself but as a by-product.

"Would Paul White have written this brochure?" I asked. If it wasn't unethical or immoral, it did nonetheless seem slightly unprofessional. Doctors, after all, do not write broadsides for beer companies. For life insurance companies, perhaps, or Blue Shield; maybe for a drug house, and even, now and then, in praise of wine. But beer was reaching a bit.

"Would Paul White have written this brochure?"

The question hung up like a slow curve ball ready to be hit out of the park. I was asking for a reason to write it. Prove to me that a physician of any stature would write this pamphlet.

The man from the beer company leaned forward. "Doctor," he asked, "why do you write these columns?" He had ignored the doctor and addressed himself to the writer. He had made the right move.

"To be read, of course." Every writer writes to be read, to remind people he has been here, to be remembered, to leave something behind.

The beer man had me, and he knew it. He waited another second or two, and then launched the harpoon.

"We are prepared," he said. "to print a half-million copies of this pamphlet."

The struggle was over. He had landed me. Paul White would have written a brochure on running that reached that many people—a half-million waiting to listen, to be instructed. And any writer would burn candles for that many minds and hearts to reach.

I said, "Okay, I'll do it."

Doing what is right is easy once you decide what is the right thing to do. The first rule in making that decision is, "Never do anything just for the money." Now, I can tell my friends at the beer company that I would have done that brochure for nothing.

Back before running became a phenomenon and Jim Fixx was still at work on his *Complete Book of Running*, he came to interview me. We talked about running and my writing, and he brought up the success of my own book, *Dr. Sheehan on Running*. Why, he asked me, had the book sold so well?

It was his idea that my book had something of the quality of that perennial best-seller, Izaak Walton's *The Compleat Angler*. People who have absolutely no interest in fishing continue to read this discourse on "The Contemplative Man's Recreation." They are simply caught up by the author's enthusiasm and encyclopedic knowledge about what many would consider a trivial subject.

In retrospect, it is clear that Fixx's book is the present counterpart of *The Compleat Angler*. His book is a compendium of all the information you would ever need to become a runner. Fixx is a fine journalist and has in addition a personal involvement, a bias, a zest that journalists are not supposed to have—or at least not show. He is an enthusiast, a true believer, a worthy successor to Walton. His book will stand.

The success of my book (I would include *Running and Being* as merely a logical extension of the first and this current book as a further development) is due not to facts but to feelings. The enthusiasm is there, God knows. I am also a true believer. But all the research, all the information is concerned with one individual: myself.

My book is not journalism; it is a journal. It is about the *feel* of being a runner, the feel of growth, the feel of control, the feel of being at home in what I am doing.

Everything we experience, we should be able to put into words. How often have we said that an event, an encounter with ourselves or others was indescribable

—and then found that someone had described it? How often have we had sensations, feelings and emotions for which we could not find adequate words— only to come across their perfect expression while browsing through a book?

Only by putting feelings into words can I possess them. Only by finding the absolutely right words can I transmit the feelings to the reader. I try to express the actual experience as clearly as I can, and hope the reader can feel the reverberation.

Remember that I, too, am a reader, and I know when a writer has bent himself out of shape in a desperate effort to capture those moments of being and becoming. When finally the best words emerge in the best order, the writer and the reader are joined. There is no more intimate relationship. What began as a writer talking to himself now becomes a dialogue with the reader.

Thoreau, who walked alone, now takes daily walks with me. Emerson, who was so reserved in conversation that he drove his friends into a fury, opens himself willingly in my company. Other loners freely admit me to their most private thoughts.

These are the writers who stir me up, give me hope, make me aware of life. They awaken me to my past and raise my consciousness to my present potential. Then, day by day, layer after layer, they lead me to the discovery of myself.

I read Emerson as he read others—sentence by sentence, year after year. Each year, I underline some thought that unbelievably I missed the year before. It is the underlining that gives it away. It is not the sort of underlining I did in school, marking passages most likely to be asked about in a quiz. No, this underlining is done because the writer has illuminated my life just as a bolt of lightning illuminates a landscape. There is a shock of recognition, a realization that this is exactly the way it is.

A book can never be written so badly, said Mark Twain, that someone won't still claim it saved his life. The letters I receive suggest that my book, despite the quality of its writing, has indeed had an impact on some people's lives. If nothing else, it has offered a validation of their own experiences. My pilgrim's progress has been matched by the progress of every pilgrim among my readers.

When someone asks me to sign one of my books, and I find it dog-eared and underlined; when a runner tells me that reading my book is like looking in a mirror; when someone says that whole paragraphs of the book had been written in his mind before he saw my words in print, then I know happiness. I have a feeling that I must write another book to express.

On a promotional tour for an earlier book, my life became a series of TV talk shows, radio interviews and luncheons with book critics. It seemed as if every minute I was asked a question. And since the people I met are good at what they do, the questions were usually probing ones.

"Why another book on running?"

"Why a book so full of quotations?"

"Why a book at all?"

Sometimes, I just smiled and said, "You're right,"

and ordered a beer. But that is not what book promo-
tion tours are for. So mostly I gave the answers which
apply to this book as well as my others.

My book is a "why" book on running, not a "how"
book. It is filled with other people's sentences because they have already said that particular thought
incomparably better than I could. It is filled with contradictions because life is filled with contradictions. It
is not a book at all. It is a journal—a series of dis-
patches from the front lines, a pilgrim's progress written, appropriately, on the run.

My book, you see, is not about running. It is about
doing your thing. It is about what happens when you
do your thing. My thing is running. You could take
this book and substitute your thing, and it would read
just as well.

The trouble with most books is that they try to prove
something. They present a theory, and then proceed
to give logical and rational reasons why it is so. The
book then ends by giving you the final answer. It ex-
hausts the subject, at least until the second edition.

No wonder when Frank Shorter was asked if he had
written a book, he answered, "No, when you write a
book you are finished."

Mine is not yet a book. It has no conclusions. There
are no answers, no solutions. It is filled with my characteristic ambiguity, my pervasive ambivalence, my
sudden enthusiasms and equally sudden defections.

When a reviewer complains that my book is filled
with contradictions, I am pleased. A book still in the
writing, like a life still in the living, should be filled
with contradictions and uncertainties, evasions and

half-truths. But it should also be filled with the sudden illuminations, the most personal of disclosures, the utterly revealing confessions.

I write about the only subject on which I am an expert: myself.

"The self that lives in my body," wrote D. H. Lawrence, "I cannot finally know."

What I must do, however, is try with all my might, even though I know that major questions will go unanswered.

Giving a lecture is like running a race. I am never sure how well I will do. I always have a slight feeling of dread, the nagging worry that this one will be a disaster. So I approach every talk as I would a race. I fast. I warm up. I get myself psyched. When I get up to speak, I want to feel lean and hungry and loaded for bear.

I eat lightly that day and not at all during the three or four hours before the lecture. If I am the after-dinner speaker, my meal goes untouched. Food and drink slow my synapses ever so slightly. I seem to be on a one-second delay. I lose the quickness of mind I need once the speech gets underway.

Another essential in this preparation is an hour's run. Coleridge once said that you will never fail in a talk after a ten-mile walk. I know what he meant. This warmup run reaches beyond the second wind of my body to the third wind of my mind. After a half-hour or so, I begin to see the theme of my talk and the direction it will take. Then this sketchy mental outline becomes fleshed out with examples and experiences that gradually surface in my consciousness.

"In any man's head," writes William Gibson, "the voices of the past are infinite, the undigested odds and ends of his lifetime, a bedlam of sights and sounds and touches of the world since his first breath."

Gibson is right. The place where I find that treasury is running on the roads. Then, I use it for my talk.

You would think I could give the same talk each time. I would like to, especially when I have had one go exceptionally well. But it's impossible. Memorizing never works.

I had a high school teacher who told me, "You can't think and remember at the same time." If I try to duplicate a past triumph, I am reduced to the D in public speaking I earned in school.

So I speak without a prepared text. I need no notes, no cue cards, no aids when I am on stage. The run has filled my stream of consciousness with all the odds and ends, sights and sounds relevant to my theme. I am now so filled with my subject I just have to get it out.

Sometimes as I enter the hall before the talk, a person will come up to me and say, "I'm very interested in hearing what you are going to say." And I will reply quite honestly, "So am I." When things go well, that is just the case. I am as interested in what I am going to say as I hope the audience is. In fact, my interest ensures theirs.

A few minutes before I am to be announced, I slip out and begin pacing the corridor, trying to get back into the stream of consciousness of the morning run. It is usually then that the full realization of what is about to come finally emerges.

One reporter who saw me in this state before a talk in Boston told me she had thought to herself, "He'll never be able to speak." Yet it seems true that the more alarmed I get, the more uncertain I become, the better I do.

Even so, beginning is always difficult. On one occasion, my mind went completely blank, and the memory of that feeling of panic still haunts me. I am also a person known only to runners. Most of my listeners have no idea who I am or what I do. All they see is a nervous, scrawny-looking sixty-year-old who is about to use up some of their valuable time.

I have a defense against this. First, I admit I am nervous. This gets their sympathy. Then, I suggest that I should have brought my American Express card. That gets the first laugh. Then, I admit that jogging is boring. That gets the second laugh. From then on, it is the audience lifting me and I am lifting the audience. The more they respond, the more relaxed and digressive and original I become.

There are times when so many new and interesting ideas fill my head, I hang the talk on imaginary pegs about fifteen feet in the air off to my left and promise to come back later. Then, I pursue some interesting anecdote or incident to its conclusion. I find that I am able then to think out loud or even have long periods of silence as I follow one line of thought after another.

The audience is a partner in this enterprise. A great

deal depends upon them. Give me salesmen any time. They are listeners by profession. They also have a disdain for facts and an appreciation of rhetoric. Although they carry catalogs and samples, what they really deal in is human nature. When they talk to a prospect, they are already anticipating his reply. Give a good talk to a convention of salesmen and they will escalate it into something even better.

Technical people are a different breed. When I say something to a group of technicians, it just lays out there and they look at it for a quite a while. In the beginning, this terrified me. I thought I was doing poorly. Now, I know it is just their way.

I am able to size up the audience and know how to give the talk. Again, it is like a race. I run differently over hills and against the wind. There are some talks that are just like that.

Every once in a while, things fall into place. I have caught the absolute attention of the crowd. My timing is perfect. Every illustration I use is new and exciting. I feel virtuoso. I am willing to go on and on—and the audience wants me to. In the end, I am never sure what I have said. All I can recall is the enthusiasm and the exhilaration. I know for forty minutes or so these people and I have entered each other's mind and hearts.

Then comes the applause, surely one of the most positive affirmations any creature can give another— and then, every once in a while, that strange and wonderful and spontaneous union of performer and audience, a standing ovation. For that, there can be only one fitting reaction: the clenched fists over the head indicating that we are all winners. Then, I give the audience a standing ovation.

Unlike the race, they are not spectators. They are part of the performance.

Part Four

The Spirit

I was in the final mile of the cross-country race when I heard him coming up on my shoulder. We were part of a rather small field, perhaps eighty in all. Only a few were accomplished runners. Most had only lately come to see the benefits of running. For them —and I'm sure for him—a five-mile race was a new experience.

When he came abreast of me, I could see he was a young lion—my superior by two inches of height and forty pounds of bone and muscle.

As he went by, I called out, "Way to go! You're looking great!"

I tried then to hang on, to stay on his shoulder and use his pace. It was no use; he was too strong. But what I did get was an impetus to try harder. Until he challenged me, I had been running to survive, thinking I was doing the best I could do.

Now, I discovered reserves I had not suspected were there. When I finished, far behind him, I was clocked in my best time of the year.

Such encounters are the rule rather than a rarity in running. They embody the essence of the racing experience. The young man, nevertheless, found my encouragement almost incomprehensible. Later, he told my son that I had blown his mind. The idea that an opponent would urge you to beat him seemed an impossibility. He became so psyched up, he said, he ran better than he had thought possible. Runners, he decided, were marvelous people.

He is right, of course. We runners *are* marvelous people. But we weren't marvelous before we began running. We were like everyone else. We wanted to get things for nothing. We had the tendency to blame others when things went wrong. We saw life as a negative-sum game where there is only one winner, where it is you against me.

I wasn't a runner long before I began to see that I had it all wrong. When I became a runner, I stopped expecting anything for nothing. I discovered that I could go just so far (about one block) without training.

Now, I am in control of what I do. What I do is me, no one else. In a race, my performance is my concern, not yours. I wish you well. In fact, the better you do, the better I will do as well.

That, I have come to see, is the true nature of competition. The Latin root of the word is *petere*—to go out, to head for, to seek. The *com* is doing it together, in common, in unity, in harmony. Competition is simply each of us seeking our absolute best with the help of each other. What we do magnifies each other, inspires each of us. The race is a synergistic society where what accrues to one accrues to all, a society in which everyone can be a winner.

When I live in such a society, if only for five miles, I learn that winning and losing is a process going on inside me. I find it unintelligible to cheat anyone or to be diminished by the performance of another. Compensation is the law of the universe. Pick what you want and pay for it. Don't ask for anything; earn it. There are no alibis.

What makes this easier is that the race is a contest. When I came to understand this, I realized how running could take me, a quarrelsome, contentious, selfish, unsympathetic human being, and make me fairly acceptable to my fellows and myself.

Contest, you see, is also a word that has a Latin root. It means "testify with." The other runners in a race are witnesses to what I do. The corollary of that statement, however, is that I am under oath. I am pledged to do my best.

In the final analysis, it is the oath that makes the difference. It makes me resist the tendency to cheat on myself, to trim the least bit, to slow down before the finish. In the last stages of the race, when along with everyone else I am wondering *why*, I remember I have given my word of honor. I am reminded that each of us shares a common oath.

That is why there is so much support in the ranks. We are all seekers, going toward a common goal; not opponents but witnesses.

At the 1978 Falmouth Road Race, after Bill Rodgers had led for the first three miles, the second-place runner said, "Bill, you're doing all the work. Let me lead for a while."

If the world was a race, it might work.

14

The Self

A reader who also runs wrote to me of his concern about my focus on self.

"The danger I see in this," he said, "is that unless prodded further, one's growth can end there. We can become a 'healthy animal' but an incomplete human being; have a fitness state of 100 and a social I.Q. of zero. The truth is that we *owe*. If we give an hour or two of the day to self, we clearly owe meaningful time to others in our work and social relationships."

This runner sees running as the beginning and the maintenance of life. But for him, complete living requires interacting with and serving others. He presented the hope that, as surely as we have evolved as runners, we will also evolve as social beings.

There are others who have taken the same view of the selfishness of runners. James Fixx, writing in

Newsweek, said much the same thing. Runners, he wrote, are incorrigible loners who, far from being troubled by their solitude, revel in it. Fixx conceded the inevitable physical improvement, and he agreed that runners become more stable emotionally, more confident and self-sufficient. But it is this very self-sufficiency which he considered "the opposite of commitment to the human community, which is the heart of the religious impulse."

That may be the conventional wisdom: Love thy neighbor, or at the very least treat everyone as if he were your brother-in-law. For most people, it would seem that religion involves other people. We must work out our salvation with and for the people who surround us.

But there are other ways to look at it. William James defined religion as "the feelings, acts and experiences of individual men in their solitude, as they stand in relation to whatever they may consider divine."

Aldous Huxley pointed out that we work out our salvation in different ways. There are, he said, three paths to salvation: the path of devotion, the path of works and the path of knowledge. Which one we take depends upon, and indeed is determined by, our own peculiar temperament and personality.

Running is not a religion. It is, however, a way of becoming an adult. It is a path to maturity, a growth process. Through it, I am prodded to go further, to grow more, to become a complete human being. I have not yet—and perhaps never will—come to where I can let my life depend on works and devotion.

Mine depends on knowledge, which begins with knowing myself.

I am not a joiner; I will not become involved. It is not that I don't want to contribute; I simply must be allowed to contribute in my own way. That way is alone—either alone on the roads or at the typewriter, or alone on the stage separated by that immeasurable distance between the podium and the first row of spectators.

That is normal for a writer and a runner. "Like many writers," someone described a novelist, "he was a cold man."

I am in many ways a cold man. I am secretive and withdrawn, no matter how open I appear in my writing and speeches. William Gibson speaks of that paradox in his *A Season in Heaven.*

> The writer can be, and at close quarters often is, unfeeling in his relations with his fellow citizens—and yet simultaneously possesses in a measure beyond any of them the social tact to move their hearts.

We each have a role to play—our own. The contemplative, even a minor-league one, has a place. Aquinas made a point of that. "It is necessary for the perfection of human society," he wrote, "that there would be men who devote their lives to contemplation."

Huxley said of the mystic, "By instinct, he remains solitary, and in the contemplation of the infinite feels himself absolved from duty to his neighbor."

The neighbor, however, may not feel the same. My running is not easily understood by those who are "people" people—those with a natural amiability and care for others. They want and give affection freely, and express their emotions without embarrassment. They are generous and kind, and for them salvation has more to do with their relationships with others than with their own destiny.

I understand these "people" people and know how important their works are. But I am not one of them. That's why I feel most at home and at peace when I run.

I am—just as you are—a unique, never-to-be-repeated event in this universe. Therefore, I have—just as you have—a unique, never-to-be-repeated role in this world. Mine is a personal drama for which I am at once author, actor and director.

Unfortunately, this perception comes late in life. It was something I knew as a child—not clearly, of course, but nevertheless with certainty. My life as a child was my own. It was filled with the play and invention, the energy and intensity, the humor and intelligence that becoming the person you are demands.

But all too soon, we become members of the herd. We learn herd rules, herd regulations, herd morality, herd ethics. We become part of society. Society must be preserved, so we accept the obligations it imposes.

Others have raised questions about this necessity. "Are we sent here," asked Thoreau, "to do chores and hold horses?" The answer, says society, is yes. Work has to be done. And if work is not available, then make-work has to be devised. We must be kept busy.

The idle mind begins to think, the idle body begins to play, and that is dangerous for the herd.

In such moments, those childlike moments, we may see ourselves as we are and recognize the life we should live. Some happy few have these revelations early. But most of us submit to the herd with little resistance. We behave docilely until we have fulfilled our obligation to procreate, until we have used our productive years in support of the institutions that keep society on an even keel.

But then what? The forties have arrived. The herd no longer needs us, nature no longer protects us, the race no longer cares. We are on our own. We have served our purpose.

What then are the prospects? Wonderful! Perhaps even better than wonderful. We can now return to the play and invention, the energy and intensity, the humor and intelligence we knew as children. The pressures that made us supportive of the herd are dying out. Each of us is feeling the urges that make us different rather than the same. Each of us is sensing the infinite varities of body and mind, of values and temperament that make us unique.

And with that comes the knowledge that the chores are over. There are no more horses to be held. We know now about the herd. We need no longer be bound by those rules, need no longer act out those roles. Somehow, we will find the strength and the courage and the insight to make our own rules, to act out our own drama.

That is the paradox. In what others consider the twilight years, we will be more than we ever were before. At a time when we are supposed to take to the easy chair and be content with serenity and a large book, we are transformed with energy. We have a vigor and a toughness youth cannot match, and for the first time since our childhood we know how to play.

Why must this all wait until we are forty? It need not, I suppose. It just happened that way in my case, but I am a slow learner and a creature of habit. For you, it might be different. Lightning may strike when you are twenty-one or not until you are seventy. Today may be your day to leave the herd.

Just before the halfway point where we were to turn for home, he passed me. I knew than I was beaten. The Marcellus Gorge 10,000-Meter Run goes out and back on the same road. The race is easy going out, being mostly downhill, but then gets very difficult coming back because of the uphill stretches.

"The first five kilometers may be the fastest you will ever run," my friend Tom Homeyer had told me. "The second five kilometers will probably be the slowest."

This runner had beaten me at my best, running downhill. There was no way I could take him going back. There was a chance, of course, that he was not in my age-group. He was fifty for sure, but maybe not yet sixty. The first over-sixty I knew was Arnie Briggs, an old-timer I'd run with for years. He was in his first race since some Achilles surgery months back, and his leg was still a little shrunken. Arnie was safely far behind me.

This unknown of unknown age kept moving away from me as we went home against those hills. I never gave up. I kept him in sight. There was even a point a mile from the end when he seemed to falter and I got within striking range. But then came the finish. I had done my best, but he had done better.

When they posted the results, I saw that he was fifty-five. So it had not mattered. I would get the beer mug with the gold medal for the sixty-and-over category after all. Then, I looked at my name just a few places down and saw they had gotten my age wrong. George Sheehan, fifty-eight.

I was studying this mistake when Tom came up and told me about the fifty-five-year-old who had beaten me. He was the local fifty-and-over champion and a great favorite among the runners. He had trained for the past three months for this race and for the possibility of beating me.

Tough luck, I thought. I could straighten this out quickly enough. Just a matter of seeing the meet director. Then, I would point out the error to the officials, tell the local hero he had beaten an old man no longer in his division and take the sixty-and-over beer mug away from Arnie.

I had just enough class to keep my mouth shut—not enough, however, to keep it shut permanently. An hour later, driving back to the hotel, I told Tom. "They had my age wrong, you know. I'm sixty." I had to get it out. But earlier, I had been in a situation that asked the question, "What is this racing about?" and I had given the right answer. I had been given an opportunity and seized it.

There are moments like this when I feel I possess that elusive quality known as class. More frequently,

I am certain I don't. But I am aware that it is always available to me. Anyone can have class. It's character is nonetheless elusive.

In talking about class and in trying to define it, one runs the risk of sounding silly and snobbish. For one thing, not only is class difficult to define, it is much more evident in its absence. Since part of class is not boasting about it, the no-class people stand out. For every class athlete you see, you can name any number of spoilsports, showboats, alibiers and cheaters.

Some say class is simply grace under pressure. Others extend it to mean those qualities Frost wrote of after an All-Star game: prowess, justice, courage and knowledge. There are some people, they say, who go through life the way DiMaggio played center field.

The Greeks have a word for it. *Arete* means the best. *Arete* also contains the idea of something, whether it be an object or a creature, doing exactly what it was made for. *Arete* means being the absolute embodiment of what it was designed to be. It is not being better than something else; it is the best of what it is. *Arete* is me being the best possible George Sheehan.

From *arete* comes the word aristocrat. It was the aristocrat who fulfilled in every respect the human design. The Greeks, who saw themselves as the playthings of the gods, were uncompromising on that issue. They settled for no less than a totally integrated person. Harmony of body, mind and spirit was their notion of class.

The important thing about actions is not what you do but the way you do it. "Every calling is great," said Oliver Wendell Holmes, "when greatly pursued." It is the old refrain all over again. Have no care for the outcome. Play the game to the hilt. Show a little class.

The great ones, whether they are mechanics or cardiologists, waiters or housewives, always do. They have all those virtues and qualities that go with class. They also have faith—faith in themselves, faith in what they are doing, faith in those they do it with. They believe the way they do something matters, and in the long run that is all that matters.

The distinction between life lived as a success and life lived as a failure, as I see it, is a matter of class. And though that word is frequently abused, I believe it does touch on something important in both the value and style of a runner's life. Class is a product of body and mind and spirit. I suspect that for me it begins with an all-consuming desire to do my best, a compulsion that everyone has felt from time to time for different activities. My task is to extend it to everything I do. I am, for instance, highly motivated in my writing and my running, but not nearly as much in my other roles and functions.

In my early days as a writer, I wrote my weekly column Tuesday night after supper. It usually had been percolating in my head for about a week, but the actual writing took about five to six hours. This meant that some member of the sports staff would be sitting late into the night, waiting restlessly for my copy. Finally, he would say, "C'mon, Doc. Everything doesn't have to be a masterpiece."

He was wrong. I want everything I write to be a masterpiece. "The true function of a writer," said

Cyril Connolly, "is to produce a masterpiece, and no other task is of any consequence."

Of course, it will be my kind of masterpiece, to be compared only with my best previous effort. And this goes for my races and my encounters with other people. They should all be masterpieces. Every day should, in fact, be a masterpiece. It is the realization of this, the enthusiasm aroused by this possibility, the exhilaration when it occasionally happens, that is at the root of class.

I saw it in a race. I ran in a two-person, six-mile relay at Lake Takanassee. The race was eight laps around the lake, which is three-quarters of a mile in circumference. We alternated, doing four laps each, going at a pace which in effect made each loop of the course a separate race.

The teams were picked out of a hat, so each group had a wide range of ability. This disparity became immediately evident, and by the time that my partner Susan had touched me off the second time, the runners were spread almost completely around the lake. Another leg, and it was impossible to tell which of the fifty teams was leading and which was last.

Each runner was now in a private little hell that interval three-quarters become, and only our partners and God cared where we were or how fast we were running. Yet as I stood there each time Susan came in, I could see in her face—and in the face of every runner making the relay exchange—an absolute and total involvement in this painful effort. There wasn't a runner there who hadn't accepted the commitment that goes with the notion of class: Do your best, knowing full well, of course, there was little chance to win or receive any recognition for your efforts.

It would have been easy to trim, to ease off, to take advantage of the fact that no one was observing you. But class will not be bought off.

15

The Others

I like running because I am in control. I control the pain. I control the stress. I can endure, it seems, almost any amount of pain as long as I am in charge.

My difficulty begins when I lose that control, when other people enter my environment. They are the primary source of my external and even internal stress. To effectively deal with them, my own resources are not enough. I must seek situations that contain support and affiliation and cohesion. What I need, as do all of us, is care and affection, assurance of my value, my worth. I need the feeling of belonging. I need to act in concert with others.

Like most runners, I seek that support and affiliation and cohesion in myself or my books or a single friend. No matter how many people are around, I am a hermit still, but like Emerson, I have come to know this is not enough. When his wife and family were away for a few days, he found the solitude tedious and dispiriting.

"Let us not wrong the truth and experience," he said, "by standing too stiffly on this cold doctrine of self-sufficiency."

When self-sufficiency is not enough, when people are necessary, I turn to the race. There, the people become *my* people. They turn the race into what Hans Selye calls "eustress," a stress which has good effects rather than bad.

My fellow runners support me by liking me, even loving me—at the least, wanting me to run my best. They join with me in a common identification, a common interest, a common experience. In the race, we are members of one body, each of us pursuing his individual goal but in a state of synergy where what is good for one is good for everyone. Whatever any runner does magnifies us all. The slowest contributes equally with the fastest.

Take, for instance, the day I ran in Central Park with 6,000 other people in the Bloomingdale-Perrier 10,000-Meter Run. As I strolled with my family across the sheep meadow toward the start, a middle-aged woman in a warmup suit ran up to me and exclaimed, "I love you, Dr. Sheehan."

What she really loved was running, the runner she had become, the person she had found herself to be. She loved me because I had tried to put into words what she felt, yet could not quite express.

From time to time, other runners would stop stretching and jogging to come over and express similar sentiments. We lovers of solitude had discovered we really did like each other.

In the race, there was more good fellowship. We took time from the business at hand to offer greetings, good wishes, encouragement, advice, even congratulations. In the course of the race, when I found the going tough, a runner one-third my age said, "Relax, Dr. Sheehan, relax."

I did. It worked a minor miracle. I soon left him behind and began to pick up one runner after another, more often than not getting an encouraging word: "Looking strong," "Keep it up," "Take it in, Doc." Some, of course, were silent, lost in their own problems. But no one saw me as a threat or a measure on his performance. The well-wishers were simply letting me know how they felt about a fellow runner.

My world of running—and my wonder in it—must open to include other people. It means a loss of control, but I am willing to take that risk, willing to chance chaos, because once in a while the magic is there. For a brief time, we are all lovers and friends, if only for a 10,000-meter race in Central Park.

A spectator kept me from quitting the three-mile race at Takanassee Lake. I was struggling through the final yards of the third three-quarter-mile lap when I heard someone shout, "You'll never feel any worse than you do now."

I immediately took heart. My body felt as bad as ever, fighting for every breath, arms and legs clad in lead, unable to move with speed or coordination. Yet suddenly I knew I would finish that lap, and even the fourth and final loop around the lake would be manageable.

My friend, whoever he was, had convinced me. He could have yelled something stupid like, "Come on, move up!" or "Go get them!" or something logical like, "Relax!" or "Use your arms!" But he knew exactly what I felt and what I feared. He was the perfect spectator: kind and interested and competent, speaking from his heart as well as his head.

The perfect spectator is, in a sense, a hypnotist. Under the relentless stress of a race, the runner may actually reach a state that approaches hypnosis. Communication on a rational level is not always possible or even desirable. Orders, if received, most often achieve negative results. Efforts to influence actions which are reflex and automatic can be counterproductive. The runner needs most of all to relax. But a "relax" shouted as a command from the sidelines will rarely be of any help.

The spectator should talk to the runner as you talk to a child: Let him know you know; praise; reassure; give hope; be realistic but confident.

I heard my man and found the strength to go on. He was right. The fourth lap wasn't any worse. I had reached a plateau of fatigue and pain and exhaustion. I even passed two runners, and two other runners passed me. We were all in the same extremity. We had reached the limits of our physiology. What served us best now was any device that helped conserve energy.

We runners need people who generate a feeling of belief and confidence and hope, who know the right thing to say at the right time. This time, it was, "You'll never feel any worse than you do now."

I was sprawled on the floor of the B. M. C. Dirfee High School gymnasium along with the 350 other runners and their families and friends. The first annual Fall River 10-Mile Run was now history. The awards ceremony was about to begin, and, as usual, I hoped to be one of the winners.

I noted with some apprehension that there were only a dozen or so trophies to be presented. Still, I had finished fortieth and run a good time on a course with two very tough hills. Surely there is medal up there, I thought, for a sixty-year-old who did that.

I am, as you can see, a pot-hunter, a sixty-year-old adolescent with a lust for trophies. If there is anything I like better than running a good race, it is running a good race and then capturing a trophy to prove it.

In the sweet afterflow of that painful struggle to the finish, there is nothing more pleasant than hearing my name called out for a prize, nothing more satisfying than making my way, with just the right mixture of pride and nonchalance, through the crowd to the awards table, and then modestly accepting my trophy.

You might think that fifteen years in the sports world would have made me more mature and sophisticated—or at least more jaundiced—about these rewards for performance. Not so. It is true that I now save only the plaques, and recycle the trophies to other meets and races. But I take that inscription plate and mount it on the dashboard of my car so I can see it daily. There, it takes its place along with other me-

mentos of such races as the 1974 Pernod Winter Series, the 1978 Atlanta Mini-Marathon and the 1979 Asbury Park Polar Bear Meet.

Up on stage the Fall River trophies were disappearing at an alarming rate. The first three went to the winner and the two fellows who followed him. Then came the first woman, who accepted the trophy and the applause with beaming face. She was a high school student, and trophies were still new to her.

I recalled a race on a Fourth of July weekend in Dennisport on Cape Cod. The high school auditorium stage was a smorgasbord of trophies and alternate selections of merchandise contributed by town businessmen. There were transistor radios, barbecue sets, alarm clocks, pottery, and any number of attractive prizes. Yet when the younger runners were called to the stage in the order of their finish and allowed to make their own selections, they headed straight for the trophies.

Our presentations continued—one for the first male Fall River runner to finish, then one for the first female Fall River runner to finish. The prizes were dwindling down to a precious few.

"First runner over forty years of age," the meet director called out. I waited hopefully while they consulted the results sheet. It was not for me. A forty-six-year-old had beaten me by over two minutes; no way I could have taken him. That knowledge helped. I might have blamed myself had it been only a few seconds. I always try my best, but when a trophy is at stake, I can sometimes summon up a little extra.

That brought to mind a race two years back where

they had 140 coffee mugs as prizes for 1,000 runners. No categories, no age groups, nothing for being a woman; just fire the gun and the first 140 back get mugs. I have never run in a more competitive race. No one would give an inch the whole way. It was five miles at flank speed. I swung into the last mile addressing my body in the third person, warning it of the consequences should it bring me in 141st. I lasted to the finish, desperately reaching for the card the official was holding out to me. Then, I looked at it and saw the number 137. For that one moment, I was the happiest man in the world.

"The first doctor." The announcer paused, glancing at his notes. This was my last, best chance. But the name he called was not mine. A young cardiology resident had taken me by just over a minute.

There had been a time when I was the class performer of the medical profession. My first year in Boston I beat the two other physicians in the race and the *New York Times* gave me the "Golden Scalpel Award." Now, I am simply one of thousands of doctors who have discovered running.

There were only two trophies left on the table. But trophies or not, I consoled myself, the weekend would stand. I had spoken to the runners the night before, discussed our responsibility for our own health, talked about our duty to squeeze the best out of what we were born with, lectured on my obligation to become the best possible—whoever I am. Running did that the natural way through joy and struggle, I assured them. Through happiness and suffering, we come to love this playful purifying discipline.

The announcer was reading the inscription on one of the two remaining trophies. "The youngest finisher," he called out. A proud eight-year-old marched up to the table, received the award and then marched back to an admiring family.

There was only one left. I suddenly knew what the category was to be, and knew also that I wanted no part of it. I squirmed down in my seat, trying to get out of sight.

I heard the words, "The oldest finisher." There was a pause, and then the winner was announced—a man of fifty-seven years. Someone off to the side disagreed. "Dr. Sheehan is at least sixty," he protested. "He should get the trophy."

The correction was made. I had won by being born in 1918, by starting and finishing. I had finally won a trophy I didn't really want.

Then, I recalled a question Satchel Paige used to ask: "How old would you be if you didn't know how old you were?" And I knew the inscription on the trophy meant nothing. They had been conned by my age into giving a trophy for old age to one of the youngest runners in the room.

16

The Faith

I was on a radio show discussing exercise with a woman who did not exercise. "The spirit is willing," she told me, "but the flesh is weak."

I had, of course, heard the excuse many times before. But for the first time, it occurred to me that the opposite was true. The flesh is willing; it is the spirit that is most often weak. Our bodies are capable of the most astounding feats. But the horizons of our spirits do not reach beyond the TV, the stereo and the car in the garage.

The flesh is not only willing; it is eager for action. The flesh is filled with everything our spirit lacks: strength and energy, endurance and stamina. We come from a breed that crossed continents on foot and trekked from pole to pole. Even now, we see housewives running marathons, stockbrokers in Outward Bound, retired executives climbing Everest.

We are of a flesh that asks for more and more challenges, that seeks one frontier after another. What is missing is not physical energy. The fuel is there, waiting to be ignited. We need some spark to light the fires, something to get us into action.

From the moment we wake up in the morning, we cop the plea that the spirit is willing but the flesh is weak. We lie abed as the alarm clock, the radio and the family take turns trying to get us up. Still, we remain immobile until the last possible minute. Yet how many calories does it take to overcome inertia and get out of bed? Whose bodies are so exhausted that they can't get their feet on the floor? I can plead that I'm in a semi-coma, not yet ready for coordinated action, but similar scenarios recur throughout the day. The body is ready, willing and able, but the spirit is becalmed. Where there is no emotion, there is no motion, either.

What is missing is the spiritual energy called *enthusiasm*. It is from lack of enthusiasm that the failures of the spirit multiply during the day. When we are enthusiastic, we develop a determination to equal the endurance of our muscles, a fortitude to match the courage of our hearts and a passion to join with the animal strengths of our bodies.

To succeed at anything, you need passion. You have to be a bit of a fanatic. If you would move anyone to action, you must first be moved yourself. To instigate, said Emerson, you must first be instigated. I am aware of this every time I lecture. For an hour before the talk, I can be seen walking alone, muttering to myself, gradually building myself to a fever pitch so I will find it completely natural to end a talk standing on a table with nothing on but my Levis—and with the pants legs rolled to my knees.

But the spirit has more to offer than just this excitement. It gives us the motivation when the excitement is missing. The spirit is what gets us through when everything else fails. As Oxford professor Ralph Johnson points out in his paper "Factors in Human Endurance," a person's ability to survive often depends on the qualities of his personality.

The mind-body relationship is particularly striking in the historical accounts of explorers and mountain climbers, people in extreme situations and stretched to their limits and beyond. The explorer, Captain Scott, writing of one of his men, commented, "Browers came through the best. Never was there such a sturdy, active, *undefeated* man." Of Scott himself, one of his companions wrote, "Scott was the strongest combination of strong man in a strong body that I have ever known—and this because he was weak. He conquered his weaker self and became the strong leader we went to follow and came to love."

Behind the enthusiasm, behind the inspiration, behind the passion, there must be the will. We can choose. We can decide. We can *will* to do it our own way. When we do, nothing can prevail against us.

Otherwise, we are merely wishing, idle dreamers in the world of the flaccid spirit. We must want something and want it badly—want it with the zeal and passion and enthusiasm of a Don Quixote or a missionary. Then, we will suddenly find ourselves in motion, with a clear focus on our goal. Once moved, the spirit and the flesh are like a matched team of horses, each asking more of the other. Fused by the will for that brief and wonderful moment, the flesh and the spirit become one.

When Viktor Frankl was in a German concentration camp, he made a pact with another prisoner. Every day they would tell each other a funny story. Every day they would find a joke in their experience in that hell that was Auschwitz. Incredible as it seems, they were able to do just that.

What Frankl and his friend instinctively knew, and psychiatrists have come to believe, is that humor is one of the best ways to cope with stress. George Valiant in his *Adaptation to Life* describes eighteen basic coping mechanisms. Of all these means of preserving our psychological equilibrium, he rates humor the first, the most effective, the most mature. Unfortunately, as Valiant points out in his study of Harvard graduates, it is rarely possessed and rarely used. Even the best and brightest are lacking in this seemingly basic human capacity.

That is surprising for if we Americans take pride in anything, it is our sense of humor. Criticize anything about me, and I am likely to agree. However unattractive you consider my features, however puny you regard my body, however unsuitable you judge my dress or companions, I will make no rebuttal. Disagree with my diet, claim the time I spend on running is absurd, say I am self-centered and penny-pinching and a poor citizen, you will get no argument. But tell me I have no sense of humor, and be prepared for a battle.

Yet I suspect Valiant is right. A sense of humor is a gift that is enhanced with age. It is the refined product of years of life's bad jokes, the result of the never-ending failures and defeats that mark the aging process. The older we get, the more likely we are to become aware of what is important and what is not, to know what is first rate and what is trash. We become able to see things and people and events for what they are.

Genuine humor is like genius and play and creativity and religion. It is simply another way of looking at things. Humor scales things down to their real significance. Humor is for the most part deflating, which is good, and humbling, which is important. But it also speaks our own truth, which is essential.

That truth is an ability to see oneself in a very special way. Humor is not only to see myself as others see me. It is even more than seeing myself as only I can see me. It is seeing myself and my circumstances as God sees me. Humor is seeing myself and my life in relation to the eternal.

Humor, therefore, is a sense of proportion and perspective. Humor is the way of wisdom, and wisdom comes only from experience. Humor is the gradual discovery of who one is and what one believes. The vision that goes with humor, then, is the vision of experience. It is seeing not only reality but that "greater reality" as well. And the older you get, the more this humor enters into everything you do. A sense of humor is no more than a sense that life is a great and glorious game and I, you, we know how to play it.

Only humor, as Frankl showed at Auschwitz, allows

you to call a spade a spade. It permits you to focus on what is too terrible to be borne and still endure. But it comes only when you have a childlike hope and trust in the human condition, and a faith that does not lie about life and death and reality. And when it comes, it is a sign of growth.

George Valiant does not miss this paradox. "Hans Selye is wrong," he states. "It is not stress that kills; it is the effective adaptation to stress that permits us to live."

In that successful adaptation, we attain the fitness of the body that is health, the fitness of the mind that is wisdom and the fitness of the soul that is humor.

If I were to suggest that creativity is a major requirement for playing this game of life successfully, I suspect most readers would feel the game was already lost. Creativity seems to most of us a rare commodity, a gift given only to exceptional people.

The truth is that each one of us has this creativity. It was more evident when we were children and playing, because creativity is playful and depends on a faith in ourselves and what we are doing. It is associated, therefore, with those adjectives we use to describe children's play—spontaneous, effortless, innocent and easy.

"Almost any child," wrote Abraham Maslow, "can compose a song or a poem or a dance or a painting or a play or a game on the spur of the moment." So, I assure you, can we.

Creativity is a different way of looking at things, a different way of looking at ourselves. When we are creative, when we are at play, when we really believe in ourselves, we open ourselves to our own experiences. We discard preconceptions. We finally become aware. We begin to live.

Creativity, therefore, is a matter of seeing the ordinary as unusual, the commonplace as miraculous, the transient as eternal. It is seeing the new in the old, looking at things as if for the first time.

Not only the child and the saint, but also the athlete takes this creative view of what would strike us as routine. The spectacular things are the routine things done every day, consistently. Mainly, creativity takes the routine and makes it important, makes it worthwhile.

Joe DiMaggio, they say, never threw to the wrong base in his entire career. Was that merely reflex? Of course not. To accomplish that record, each individual throw had to be made with the intensity, fervor and freshness of the very first throw. DiMaggio transformed an activity that could have become routine into a creative challenge.

Andrew Wyeth was another man who had a creative response to familiar things. "I'm not much for the new thing or the new object," he said. "I like to go back again and again, because I think you can always find some new things. I'm actually bored by fresh things to paint. To make old things seem fresh is much more exciting to me."

If Wyett can discover more in the everyday and the familiar, so can we. For myself, I now see that there are innumerable opportunities for creativity. All I need is the faith, the confidence, the ability to let go, and the attitude of play. Then, I can create—when I come together with my family or friends, when I write, when I run, or when I just sit on the beach and look at the sea. The most routine, the most simple act can be a creative event.

"Run into peace," wrote Meister Eckhart, the fourteenth-century mystic. "The man who is in the state of running, of continuous running into peace, is a heavenly man. He continually runs and moves and seeks peace in running."

Now, one should not take the writings of a mystic too literally. They usually tell their good news in analogies and similes and other figures of speech. In this passage, I am sure Eckhart was using running as a metaphor. It represented the soul in motion. He was saying in his own way, "He who seeks God has already found Him." As had many early preachers, he was using running to help us understand the religious experience.

But Eckhart, at least for me, wrote more truly than he knew. I have discovered that "run into peace" can be understood literally as well as figuratively. For me, running is a religious experience. When I run, I actually run into peace. On my river road thirty minutes from where I began as a fallen, finite, sinful creature, I approach Eckhart's vision of the heavenly man.

By that time, I have taken the bad me and gradually stripped myself of anything that keeps me from the physical good. Running is the purifying discipline that the Greeks sought so their bodies would be fit for the gods to inhabit. When I run, I am purged. I am cleansed. I take this beautiful body entrusted to me and perfect it. I become a good body.

The mystic proceeds methodically. His progress is from purgation to illumination to union. And so it is for me in the running: purgation in movement and effort and sweat; and in that cleansing I discover myself becoming whole physically, and allowing for the possibility of further movement toward illumination and union. Because running is not only the movement of the body but is also the movement of the soul.

That movement of the soul is the essence of the religious act. That was the conclusion William James came to in his monumental work, *The Varieties of Religious Experience*. All religions, he pointed out, consist fundamentally of two parts: (1) an uneasiness, and (2) its solution. The uneasiness stems from the sense that there is something wrong with us as we naturally stand. The solution is the recognition that we are saved from wrongdoing by making connection with a higher power.

What happens, said James, is that we not only see the bad in ourselves but the good as well, and we then establish that good as our real self. We realize there is a "more" in us, a better part, and then we reach toward the supreme *more* operating in the universe.

Such description allows, according to James, for all the various religious phenomena he catalogued in his book. It allows us to understand conversions and backsliding, saints and sinners. It accounts for the exteriority of the helping power yet also our sense of union with it. And finally, it fully justifies our feelings of security and joy.

In all of this, it is the progression past purgation that becomes difficult. What we are seeking is an altered state of consciousness, a return to a wholeness that we have not had perhaps since childhood, a crossing over into the universal. To do this, we must somehow divert the rational processes. We must dispense with the having and the getting, the planning and the analyzing, the ambition and the anxiety.

Mystics do this with prayer. Meditators do it with the mantra. Researchers do it with a repetitive word. It is this repetitive word, this mantra, this prayer, William Gibson tell us in his *A Season in Heaven*, that puts a veil between us and the things of the world. And so we enter a cloud of unknowing where and only where we can encounter Him directly.

When I run, motion becomes my mantra, movement becomes my prayer. Running puts me into another reality, a world where truth can be felt but not defined. Running is the way I alter my consciousness, suspend disbelief, ascend to a new perception. But even then, the individual illumination, the experience of union cannot be programmed. We know those moments are rare and wonderful. Once experienced, however, you can never again deny their existence.

A reader who is also a poet wrote to me commenting on my answer to the question, "Can running be a religious experience?" The question that occurred to her was "Can *living* be a religious experience?"

Cannot everything we do, she asked, be a religious experience, every breath we take, every act of love, of awareness, of stretching, whether we are running the roads or in bed or in the middle of a Brahms symphony?

Having defended running, I'm inclined to agree with her. Every human act, every act that is not simply reflex or automatic is a religious—or an irreligious—act. When it is considered and voluntary and purposeful, every act is a statement about me and my universe, a confirmation of how I view my existence.

"Religion," William James said, "consists in the belief that there is an unseen order, and our supreme good lies in harmoniously adjusting ourselves thereto."

That this is available to all was pointed out by James. "The solid meaning of life," he wrote, "is always the same eternal thing—the marriage namely of some unhabitual ideal with some special fidelity, courage and endurance; with some man's or woman's pains"—and whatever or wherever life may be, there is always the chance for that marriage to take place.

Whatever we do or wherever we do it we can take that occupation and make it a vocation. We can do it in a way we will always be remembered. Unamuno writes of the shoemaker who aspired to become for his fellow townspeople the one and only shoemaker, indispensable and irreplaceable. Then, writes Unamuno, this man made the theoretical fact that each one of us is unique and irreplaceable, a practical truth.

Everything I do should speak of that belief, that adjustment. What I do is a visible sign of what I believe. My actions are the answer to the question, "What would I do if I knew what I should be doing?"

What you do earns its value from the way you do it.

When running becomes for me, as my poet friend put it, "a totally entered experience," it becomes a religious experience. I give it my body. I give it my mind. I give it the yearnings of my heart, the further reaches of my soul. From the act of running—now an act of awareness, of love, of stretching myself—comes whatever wholeness, whatever certitude I possess then and for the rest of the day.

One can, of course, obtain wholeness and certitude ready-made. There are any number of people trained and ready to tell me what is best. There is a truth already given. Why question or criticize it? Why not accept it and free myself for other activities? There is no need, and there is more than a little danger, in seeking it myself.

The answer, for me, is the suspicion that nothing that I need to know is known. There is no one who knows just how I should live and die. I must discover that for myself.

William James, who spent his life in the pursuit of truth, died with a note on his dresser stating there were no conclusions. "There is no advice to give," the note said, "no fortunes to be told. Farewell."

When I read James, however, what I see is very specific advice. There is no substitute for experience. There is no substitute for finding out for one's own self, for the personal revelation, for knowing first-hand.

When I run, that happens. The body and the spirit become one. Running becomes prayer and praise and applause for me and my Creator. When I run, I am filled with confidence and the faith that word contains. I can face unanswerable questions, certain that there are answers.

That is something my poet friend would understand. Poets see other worlds, other consciousnesses. They do not see boundaries. They can deal with contraries. They refuse limits. In the commonplace, they see the miraculous. But most of all, they disdain logic.

"Swiftly rose and spread about him," sang Whitman, "the peace and knowledge that pass all argument of the earth."

That is something even I understand. The peace and knowledge that pass all argument I do indeed know. I run and feel it rise up and spread around me. That ordinary act contains all that need be seen and heard and tasted and felt and spoken—as can anything we do each day.

The religious experience, you see, is too important to be confined to church. It must be available to me at every moment. When it is absent I am, in that sense, no longer living. I am existing. I am on life supports, outside of life, like a patient in a coma. I am unconscious, unaware of what being human means. One way to come out of that coma is to be a runner.

17

The Ends

"We live in an open universe," said William James, "in which uncertainty, choice, hypothesis, novelties and possibilities are natural."

But if the universe is unfinished, so are we. Each one of us is, in fact, an open universe. Each one of us is a microcosm of uncertainty, choice, hypothesis, novelties and possibilities. Each one of us is an unfinished person in this unfinished universe. And each one of us feels an infinite and mysterious obligation to complete ourselves and somehow contribute to the completion of the universe.

One manifestation of the preoccupation with human potential is what is happening in Marin County, California, the subject of a TV special called, "I Want It All Right Now." Marin is a "more" county—more money, more schooling, more foreign cars, more expensive houses. Marin also has more drinking, more psychiatrists, more divorces and more suicides. It is filled with people who have made it and have found that making it is not enough.

Many people in Marin are discovering the truth in the old platitudes. More is never enough. Beauty and power and success do not bring peace. To go forward, you must go back into yourself.

And they have in Marin County. The search for happiness has become the search for self. Body awareness has become a major industry. You can find there almost every one of the self-realization and self-knowledge movements. You name it, and it has moved to Marin County.

What happens in this concentration on the self is not always for the best. Obsession with the self can create chaos in individual lives and leave behind the wreckage of other people. Families, friends and lovers are frequently the victims of this complete self-absorption. Everything and everyone is sacrificed in this remaking of a human being.

The self is, of course, initially selfish. Stripped of all those social devices that permit us to live together with a minimum of discord, the self stands there naked and completely selfish. That is what the critics see—the selfishness and self-absorption of many people who move toward their goals at the expense of other people, destroying human potential rather than increasing it. Such people, they say, are not going toward meaning but away from it, not learning how to love other people but how to get along without them, not finding satisfaction in the remaking of the world but in removing themselves from it.

As usual, everyone is right—the critics and those they criticize. The human potential movement is, in the beginning, and for a long time must be, selfish. Only by going deep into ourselves can we come back with a complete and natural acceptance of our need for others. Then, what was a duty becomes a delight, what was obligatory flows from the source.

It is apparent that for many people this final stage comes only after a long period of self-discovery. It may even take a lifetime. I, for one, know that I must go through a lot more isolation and study, search and solitude before I become a social being.

In a way, it is like being a ninety golfer and wanting to be better. We have to destroy our game and rebuild it, go back to the basics and start over. But it is not easy to begin at the beginning, to give up our little securities and satisfactions. We are reluctant to do away with our minor pleasures, to leave the comfort of the status quo. We do not want to risk what we have for the unknown.

But we must take that risk. Given all this leisure and freedom, we must live up to it. Given all this time and money, we cannot stand pat. We cannot bury these assets any more than we can bury our talents. We are accountable, and we know it.

I feel that accountability every day. I am filled with what Joan Didion called "that low dread" of having to go out and better myself. I move through days filled with failure of the body and the mind and the spirit—

still trusting I am going on in the right direction, hoping that the real me is infinitely better than the acceptable me I am leaving behind.

We are always in the process of becoming. We have a commitment strongly spent or weakly kept, as Robert Frost said, to the work or career of person in progress. The original commitment may alter as we grow or be diverted by outside influences. But change or not, the commitment is there—and with it our word of honor to do what is necessary for its fulfillment.

There is no substitute, therefore, for the orthodox virtues—discipline, hard work, pleasure postponed, duty followed. We must keep our eye on the goal, keep looking at the hills.

That is the good life—coping and striving and eventually becoming the person you are, the self you were born to be. That self is the final product of a lifetime of dedication, of finding what you are good at and then doing it well.

The highest, happiest and most perfect moments of our lives are the reward for the good becoming. In our pure and dedicated drive toward the future, we are likely to be, as C. S. Lewis said, "surprised by joy." We suddenly do have it all right now. That is the paradox. Only by aiming at the future will we become lost in the present. Only be deferring gratification will we get it immediately. Happiness, we come to discover, is found in the pursuit of happiness.

I see this in everything I do. I am runner, doctor, writer—body, mind and spirit, you might say—and each I do with all my might. Let me tell you about the running.

When I am training for a marathon, I am not running for fun. I am working on my limits of pain and exhaustion, so I will do well in the race. It is a classic instance of deferred gratification.

But oddly, each workout becomes an end instead of a means. It is as Emerson said: "All that is not performance is preparation—or performance shall be." I am already part of the event I am preparing for.

Either what we do every day is important, or nothing is. In a sense, we can live our entire life every day. I see this most clearly the day of a race. Then, the full cycle is evident.

The planning, the anticipation, the anxiety, the tension, the worry that fills my life comes before every race. This is followed by the race itself, the soon-evident inadequacies, the continuing failure, the falling behind—all the while knowing pain and fatigue, suffering and despair—and finally the finish, and joy and the peace beyond understanding.

The half-marathon in Atlanta was no exception. With seconds to go, I still hadn't gotten my shoelaces quite right. Every time I adjusted them, they were too tight or too loose. And then there was the matter of what to wear. It had been cold the last two days. The temperature had hovered around freezing, and there had been a threat of snow. Now, it was warming up. There was a bright sun and no wind. I had changed my clothes three times before settling for a cotton turtleneck, a nylon shirt, gloves and a wool hat.

My world was full of uncertainties. I had forgotten to warm up, and it was now too late. I had taken a

Coke for the first time before a race and was worried about that. My stomach was full of butterflies. My mouth was dry, and my heart was speeding up in my chest. And just before the fun came an announcement: Only those who ran one hour and thirty-two minutes or better would receive medals.

So there it was, true to life even to the Final Judgement. The good news was that there was a hereafter. The bad news was that we would be separated into sheep and goats. There would indeed be an elect, the rest consigned to outer darkness with neither medals nor trophies. I stood with those hundreds. My mind, like theirs, had turned from the race to the outcome —from the living of my life to the rewards.

Every athlete knows that moment. Just before the gun, before the whistle, before the first center jump, it is that moment when all thought is about the prize, the championship, the winning and the losing. I knew it those last few seconds at Atlanta.

It took a while to lose it. Within minutes, we were into the first of what proved to be continuous hills. I am no hill runner, and with almost every yard I was passed by another runner. So added to the fear of the 1:32 barrier was the envy of those who were obviously going to break it.

Fortunately, I was unaware of what lay ahead. The man next to me was from Chicago. He had flown in the day before and driven the course in a rented car.

"There are," he told me, "three long hills."

I didn't ask him for any details. What was in sight was bad enough.

Then, the sweating began. And with the sweat came

release from the fear of the future. With the sweat came play. I was no longer threatened by the race or my fellow runners. I can best describe it, perhaps, as a feeling of control and a feeling of freedom. I suddenly felt confident in a setting of uncertainty.

The paradox of play, however, is how serious it can be. Now it was just me and those Atlanta hills fighting it out. Mostly, I fought their injustice; the distance was surely enough of a test. But I asked no mercy, enjoying the struggle, seeking to be stretched, hoping for the summit, yet never slackening the pace until the crest was passed.

By now, I had taken the nylon shirt off and stuffed it into my shorts. Gone were the hat and gloves. I had slipped the turtleneck back over my shoulders and was running bare-chested in the thirty-eight-degree weather. I felt as strong as I had ever felt in my life. I had the 1:32 barrier beaten, and I didn't really care. I had stopped counting the hills. Let them come; I was ready.

Those final miles were filled with feeling and knowing, but most of all with believing. I believed in myself, for one, and in things about me I might never be able to explain or prove; in love, the love that is born in common suffering and anguish and therefore is really pity, and in God and the hereafter.

Afterward there was a plane to catch, so I missed the awards ceremony and the Final Judgement. Not that it mattered. There's another one every day.

Epilogue

A fellow runner who is in the publishing field told me a story about meeting the wife of a former associate.

"What is Ted doing these days?" he asked.

"Training at seven minutes a mile," she said, "and looking to go under three hours in the marathon."

He still doesn't know if Ted has a job.

In running circles, such replies are standard. When a stranger asks me what I do, my reflex is to tell him my time for the marathon. The marathon, you see, is my bench mark. It is the status symbol in my community, the running community. It is my credibility factor, not only for others but for myself as well. My marathon time is in fact my most valued possession. By it, I can establish my value as a runner, and each year I raise or lower that value according to what I do in the Boston Marathon.

I tell you this so you may understand the apprehension I felt during the 1979 Boston race. The fear began soon after I had run the gauntlet of cheering women at Wellesley. Pains hit my thighs. They were those same ominous, stabbing pains in the quadriceps that are usually felt only in the final miles. I knew then I was in for a long, painful marathon—and worse, a bad time. The next thirteen miles would be filled with suffering, and with the danger that I would be reduced to walking and perhaps not finishing at all.

Before the marathon, a reporter had asked me what I expected to learn from this race. He had read something I had written about each Boston Marathon being a learning experience. At the time, I was at a loss to answer. Who knows what he will learn until it happens? I didn't know that this was to be one of my most instructive Boston Marathons.

As I ran with that constant pain, I gradually came to the realization that it was not my fault I was running a bad race. "It's not your fault, George," I kept saying to myself. "You're doing the best you can." And I was. I was running the best race I could, and I began to be proud of it.

There were times, of course, when my mind leaped forward to the finish at the Prudential Center and the image of my impending disgrace. There were times when I was reduced to a grotesque shuffle and with it the thought that I might not see my family until nightfall.

Yet even then I continued to chant to myself, sometimes loud enough for the spectators to hear, "Do your best, do your best." And I did. I was running the one and only race possible for me this day. I forgot about the final time. I forgot about everything but the running.

I finished in 3:15—four minutes slower than the previous year. but it was the best 3:15 I had ever run —not a defeat, but a victory.

Once I stopped running, I found it almost impossible to walk. And after the cramps came the chills. Someone put a sheet of metallic foil around me, and I made my way through the crowd up the escalator to the Prudential Building.

The crowds clogged the walkways and impeded my painful progress, so I went through a side door and started across the plaza at the second level. It was empty except for a woman who was standing in my path. As I approached her, I had to go down a set of three steps not more than a few inches high. The only way I could do it was by turning around and taking them one at a time, backwards. I saw that the woman was watching me very intently.

She said, "Who are you?"

That weekend, I had been a man of many identities, many selves: I had been lecturer, doctor, writer and even celebrity. Now, I was a shivering, wobbling scarecrow wrapped in tinfoil.

"Who are you?" she asked again.

"Just a runner," I answered.

Then, she leaned over and kissed me.